"Message from the Author"

I wrote A Soul to Care: A Blessing that came from Trouble to identify the social determinants for premature crime exposure and gun violence.

The screenplay is of my life story from childhood into nursing. I grew up as a GIT. GIT is an acronym for Gangster in Training. A Florida term used to describe a school age child (6 to 12 years old) entering a criminal lifestyle. A criminal lifestyle that normalizes prison and death as a reality for the young that live by The G Code.

The G Code is to commit murder or die. A GIT's mentality has been inured to think that if he wants to become someone in life, he must kill somebody or be killed. So, today's youth live by the G code, that is to commit murder or die to become someone in society.

Thank you for purchasing my book. - AG

GIT HOUND, Age 15

"A SOUL TO CARE"

A BLESSING THAT CAME FROM TROUBLE

Written By

Anthony A. Gray, MSN RN

"NURSES ARE BORN AND NOT MADE. I CAN
TEACH YOU HOW TO BE A NURSE, BUT I
CANNOT TEACH YOU HOW TO CARE."

- DR. GALE WOOLLEY

EXTERIOR CITY - AFTERNOON

A MAN is getting off the hospital
gurney and exiting from a busy city's
hospital emergency room with IVs lines
still intact. HE is walking slowly
down a street in Overtown holding onto
his IV pole, and only wearing a
hospital gown. The street is occupied
with dope pushers and dope users. THE
MAN has pronounced neck veins, swollen
feet and ankles. HE makes his way up a
dark pissy stairwell. HE knocks on the
black iron fenced door. The door has a
screen protector. THE MAN could not
see inside.

INTERIOR APARTMENT - AFTERNOON

Sitting at a table full of crack-
cocaine on a plate is a teenage drug-
dealer named GIT (Gangster in
Training). GIT responds to the knock
at the door.

        GIT - YEAH!

THE MAN slides in a one-hundred-dollar
bill through an opening in the door.

    THE MAN - Look out for me now. I
    need this.

    GIT - Man, you look crazy as
    fuck. Where you are coming from?

    THE MAN - I was in the hospital.
    I had to leave.

    GIT - What? (Angry voice) Nigga!
    Look at your neck. Your feet are
    all big and shit. What the fuck
    you got going on dog?

    THE MAN - Them doctors talking
    about my heart and shit. I'm all
    fucked up now. My nuts are
    swollen and shit! They trying to
    give me some shit but fuck that I
    need my real medicine. Now, look
    out for me.

    GIT - Nigga, I ain't got shit for
    you. Go back to that muthafucking
    hospital and get yourself checked
    out dog.

A momentarily argument occurs between
THE MAN and GIT over drugs. GIT slides
the money back to THE MAN and THE MAN
leaves. A couple of minutes later

another dope fiend knocks on the door
and slid a one-hundred-dollar bill
through an opening in the door.

GIT - Man, where the fuck did you
get this money from?

THE DOPE FIEND - GIT, let me get
four quarters.

GIT: Where that nigga at?

THE DOPE FIEND - What nigga?

EXTERIOR CITY - AFTERNOON

GIT opens the door and confronts the
DOPE FIEND.

GIT - The nigga with the
muthafucking IV pole.

THE DOPE FIEND points in the direction
down the stairwell. GIT locked the
door. Went down the stairs. Gave THE
MAN back his money and walked with him
towards the city's hospital.

THE MAN - Young blood you don't
want this money.

GIT - All money ain't good money.

THE MAN - Then, why you in this
shit for?

GIT - I was born in this shit,
and I'm made for this shit.

THE MAN - GIT, you were born in
this shit.

THE MAN pauses and looks around at the
poverty-stricken neighborhood of
Overtown. Looks back at GIT.

THE MAN - But you made for
something else.

GIT and THE MAN continue to walk and
talk towards the direction of the
hospital on a street occupied by dope
pushers and users.

INTERIOR CELL BLOCK - NIGHT

"A few months earlier"

The music plays. Gangster Rap.

The cell block is filled with fourteen
juvenile offenders. Some are playing
cards, chess, writing, and exercising.
The two correctional officers are
sitting in the chairs observing the
offenders.

The NARRATOR speaks over the music as
the music volume lowers.

NARRATOR: November 5, 2001, the night before my release. I was at the delicate age of seventeen years young. I just spent nearly a year out of my life at a juvenile correctional facility in Everglades, Florida serving time for strong-arm robbery. I had to accept the robbery charge at the time. I never took anything from the person, but I was there when the crime was being committed and in the eyes of the law, I was guilty. If I would have told authorities what really happened, then I would have had to snitch on my homeboy and snitching in the streets is a no no. I was not guilty of the robbery charge, but I was not innocent to the culture of the street life. Since my childhood, the code of the streets was embedded into my mind frame. As a teenager, I was becoming an active participant in the drug game. After being incarcerated, I was on a path to think that I have changed, but jailhouse thinking is not the same as freedom actions.

INTERIOR THE CELL - NIGHT

GIT is lying on his bunk. The music
stops.

> NARRATOR: My childhood was that
> of any other inner-city youth
> during the 1980s. Poverty and the
> exposure to street violence were
> the standard patterns of the
> ghetto in Overtown. As a child, I
> witnessed many drug transactions
> and shootings that caused my soul
> to become immune to crime.

GIT gets off his bunk.

> NARRATOR: My parents were
> teenagers when they started to
> have kids. My MOTHER was sixteen
> years old with three children
> from my FATHER, and my FATHER was
> eighteen with four children. One
> from an outside relationship.
> Teenage pregnancy was a common
> pattern on the maternal side of
> my family. My maternal
> grandmother and maternal great-
> grandmother were both teenage
> mothers. My sister, TOYA followed
> our MOTHER'S path and became a
> teenage mother at the age of
> fifteen. My brother and I
> followed our FATHER'S path and
> became involved in Dade County's
> dangerous drug game as teenagers.

GIT paces in the cell.

> NARRATOR: During my childhood, my
> FATHER was never around. Either
> he was incarcerated or involved
> in a drug war. I rarely spent
> time with my DAD. HE was twenty-
> four years old when HE got a
> twenty-five-year sentence for
> trafficking cocaine in the State
> of Florida.

The music stops.

GIT goes and looks out of the tiny
cell's window and stares up at the
stars.

> NARRATOR: My MOTHER had a lot of
> pressure to be a young single
> MOTHER in the ghetto. SHE was
> young with three kids to support
> by HERSELF. We moved to better
> neighborhoods for some time with
> the help of Section 8, but the
> culture of the ghetto was
> indoctrinated in our spirits. WE
> were troubled kids and caused a
> lot of havoc in schools and in
> the neighborhoods. My BROTHER and
> I spent a lot of our young
> teenage lives at the juvenile

detention center, and that put a burden on our MAMA'S heart. SHE did the best that she could at the time, but the pressure eventually got to her. SHE abandoned my BROTHER and I when we were fifteen and sixteen years old because we were heading down the same path as our FATHER.

EXTERIOR HOUSE – DAY

GIT is released from jail to his aunt's house. He has on an oversize white t-shirt, baggy jeans, white socks, and tan jail house slippers. He is greeted on the front porch by his relatives, BIG SAM and MON.

> MON - Look at this nigga! GIT what they do?
>
> GIT - Laughing. Nigga I'm free as fuck.

GIT gives MON a five handshake.

> BIG SAM - Laughing. I see you got some size on you fool.
>
> GIT - Hell yeah. You know how that jail shit be my nigga. Laughing.

GIT gives BIG SAM a five handshake.

BIG SAM - You on papers?

GIT - Hell Yeah, but for only
four months tho. MON you think
DEAN will let me stay here? I had
given them folks this address.

GIT was living at his AUNT DEAN'S
house when his MOTHER had abandoned
him prior to HIS incarceration.

MON - Yea, you should be good.
Can't smoke?

MON has a marijuana joint in his hand.

GIT - What's that?

MON - Dirty (marijuana lased with
cocaine).

GIT takes the joint and smokes it.

GIT - Fuck them papers!

BIG SAM - Thug life again nigga.

GIT, BIG SAM, and MON all laughing.
The music plays. Gangster Rap.

The NARRATOR speaks over the music as
the music volume lowers.

NARRATOR: My first day out. I smoked a joint, hung out with the homies, and forgot about the changes that I was going to make. Again, jailhouse thinking is not the same as freedom actions.

INTERIOR OFFICE - MORNING

The music stops.

GIT goes to Lindsey Hopkins Technical Educational Center to enroll in the GED (General Educational Diploma) program.

GIT - Good morning ma'am.

OFFICE CLERK - How may I help you?

GIT - I would like to enroll in the GED program please.

OFFICE CLERK - Okay. What is the last grade of school you completed?

GIT - I think the ninth.

OFFICE CLERK - You think?

The OFFICE CLERK has a puzzled look on her face.

OFFICE CLERK - How old are you?

GIT - I'm seventeen.

OFFICE CLERK - Seventeen! What have you been doing all this time?

GIT - Ma'am with all respect, I just got out, and I need to enroll in school as part of a probation requirement.

OFFICE CLERK - Oh, you are one of those?

GIT - Yes ma'am. I am one of those.

OFFICE CLERK - You seem so polite. I hope that you are here to make a change.

GIT - Laughs. Most definitely. But you know how it is.

The woman looks GIT into his eyes.

OFFICE CLERK - You all make it like it is. It doesn't have to be like that young man. It doesn't.

EXTERIOR APARTMENT COMPLEX — DAY

GIT went to visit his paternal grandmother, GRANNY. GIT plays the game Nick Knocking on her door.

INTERIOR APARTMENT - DAY

GRANNY is sitting on the loveseat. Watching a television show. GIT bangs on her door and ran to hide behind the tree close by the front window.

GRANNY- Who is it?

GRANNY pauses for five seconds.

GRANNY- Who is it?

No response.

EXTERIOR APARTMENT COMPLEX - DAY

GIT waited a minute then went to bang on her door again and ran behind the tree.

INTERIOR APARTMENT - DAY

GRANNY- Who is it? Who is it?

GRANNY gets up from her seat. Goes to the window but could not see anyone.

EXTERIOR APARTMENT COMPLEX - DAY

GIT waited a couple of minutes, then he banged on her door again but ducked

down at the door this time, so he
could not be seen.

>GRANNY- Who the fuck keeps
>playing at my muthafucking door?
>I'll shoot your muthafucking ass
>if you bang on this door one more
>muthafucking time.

GIT stands up.

>GIT- Laughing! GRANNY you ain't
going to shoot nothing.

>GRANNY- ANTHONY! Is that my baby?

>GIT- I just got out the joint. I
>ain't nobody's baby. What's good
>GRANNY?

GRANNY opens the front door to give
GIT a hug.

>GRANNY- My baby! Good to see you.
>I'm glad you are home. Come on
>in.

INTERIOR APARTMENT - DAY

>GIT- How have you been doing
>GRANNY?

They both sit on the love seat.

GRANNY- GRANNY has been doing
alright. Getting old is a bitch
you hear.

GIT- Laughing.

GRANNY- I missed you so much. You
know that I wanted to come see
you. But they had you so far this
time! And that STS would have
been a hassle.

GIT- I know GRANNY. I did that
time like a soulja.

GRANNY looks at GIT with tears in her
eyes.

GIT-GRANNY don't cry. What's
good? You are looking old as
usual.

GRANNY- Laughs. Nigga I am old.

GIT- Laughs.

GRANNY- Where are you coming
from?

GIT- Lindsey. Just enrolled in
the GED program.

GRANNY- Good. ANTHONY, you know
that you are very smart, and you
have a good heart. Just make the

right decisions baby. GOD has
something for you to do.

GIT- Come on GRANNY with all that
GOD talk. GOD put a nigga here to
cause trouble.

GRANNY- ANTHONY you don't steal,
and you have a good heart, baby.
That doesn't come around too
often. Especially around here.

GIT gets up and starts looking at his
DAD'S pictures on the shelf.

GRANNY- Where are you staying?

GIT- At my AUNTIE DEAN'S house.

GRANNY- You heard from your mama?

GIT- She wrote me a couple of
times. I supposed to see her this
Sunday to go and see my DAD.

GRANNY- Good. You remind me of
him so much. I miss my son. I got
to write him. You know your
parents love you?

GIT - Man that lady just left a
nigga. And my DAD has been gone
for about eleven years now. He
gonna talk that jailhouse talk.

GRANNY- ANTHONY they were young when they had y'all. I'm not making any excuses, but they did the best that they could.

GIT looks at the pictures of his FATHER with tears in his eyes. GIT always admired the stories that were told of HIS FATHER especially the gangster shooting stories.

GRANNY- You hungry?

GIT - Now GRANNY, I just came over to see you the world's oldest person (laughing), and to get a plate. You know that I am hungry. They both laugh. The music plays. Soulful gospel.

GRANNY goes in the kitchen to cook. GIT takes off his shoes, lays on the love seat, and watches television.

The NARRATOR speaks over the music as the music volume lowers.

NARRATOR- I spent a lot of my childhood going back and forth from my MOTHER'S house to GRANNY'S house. I got along with GRANNY better. SHE is my paternal grandmother. GRANNY is the

definition of a Souljah,
revolutionary, and a scholar. SHE
is a retired schoolteacher and
licensed practical nurse. SHE
helped plenty of folks in the
hood with literacy guidance,
financial management, and
positive self-help talk. My DAD
and HER had a tight relationship.
SHE advised him plenty of times
to stay away from the drug game,
but HE got involved like many
other teenagers in the 1980s. The
drug game played a huge part in
the downfall of many black
communities that were established
post Dr. King. It became an
acceptable normality for young
black men in America to
experience prison or death during
the 1990s. I guess that's why I
never really got punished for my
troubles as a teenager because it
was an expected outcome.

The music stops.

EXTERIOR POOL HALL - EVENING

GIT walks up to the pool hall entrance
to look for his brother, DAVE. He is

greeted at the entrance by an old
timer named GRAPE.

>GIT - A what's up man? DAVE
>around?

>GRAPE - Who you?

>GIT- I'm his brother.

>GRAPE - I ain't know BOBBY had
>more sons. Laughs. BOBBY is a
>mother fucker. You BOBBY'S son?

>GIT - That nigga raised us. You
>can call it that.

GRAPE walks to the iron fence door at
the entrance of the stairwell and
yells for DAVE.

>GRAPE - Yo DAVE! DAVE!

At the top of the dark stairwell is
DAVE.

>DAVE- Yeah!

>GRAPE - Some ugly ass nigga that
>look like you; is looking for
>you.

DAVE walks down the stairwell.

>DAVE - Laughs. Your old ass on
>that bullshit dog.

DAVE looks at GIT.

GIT - GIT what they do? Laughs.
You got some size on you nigga.

DAVE greets GIT with a five handshake
with a hug.

GIT - You know how that jail shit
be my nigga.

DAVE - Hell yeah! What's good
tho?

GIT - Just came from checking on
GRANNY.

DAVE - I already know. Everybody
knows you her baby and shit.
Laughs.

GIT - You on that bullshit.

DAVE - For real tho. What's good?

GIT and DAVE walk down the street.

GIT - A nigga trying to eat fool.
You feel me.

DAVE - Already know fool. That
nigga B ain't hear till later.
I'll talk to him when he gets
here.

GIT - That's a bet. Imma about to dip (leave) my nigga. I just came to holler at you and see if you can plug me in. This probation shit got a nigga on a curfew.

DAVE - Where you at?

GIT - At DEAN'S house.

DAVE - I'll pull up on you first thing tomorrow, and I'll let you know what the play is.

GIT - For show my nigga. Don't tell that nigga BOBBY I'm on probation tho.

DAVE - Got you. Luv.

GIT - Luv.

GIT gives DAVE a five handshake.

INTERIOR APARTMENT - NIGHT

A woman, SANDY is cleaning her apartment. She hears the telephone ring, and she answers the phone.

SANDY - Hello!

OPERATOR - You have a collect call from...

DAVID - DAVID.

OPERATOR - An inmate at a Florida Correctional Facility. To accept charges, press five. To decline please hang up now.

SANDY presses five on the telephone.

DAVID - Hello. Hello.

SANDY - Hello.

DAVID - A what's up?

SANDY - Nothing much.

DAVID - What are you up to?

SANDY - Same ol. Just cleaning the house.

DAVID - How's my granddaughter?

SANDY - She's fine. Getting bigger every day.

DAVID - How's TOYA?

SANDY - She's holding up. She's trying to remain strong after that boy died from a brain tumor.

INTERIOR PRISON DORM ROOM - NIGHT

DAVID is standing at the prison's phone.

DAVID - That nigga should be dead
for getting my daughter pregnant.
Shit.

INTERIOR APARTMENT - NIGHT

SANDY - There you go. Still with
the foolishness.

DAVID and SANDY argue briefly over the
phone.

INTERIOR PRISON DORM ROOM - NIGHT

DAVID - What's up with my boys?
Smiles (gold teeth).

SANDY - DAVE only comes around
when he needs something. I hadn't
seen him since the last time he
took that money out of my purse.

DAVID - Damn DAVE. What about my
lil man?

SANDY - His ass is out.

DAVID - He's coming Sunday?
Smiles.

SANDY - He says he will. I told
him to be ready early.

OPERATOR - You have one-minute
remaining on this call.

        DAVID - Look I gotta go. Make
        sure you bring him. I love you.

INTERIOR APARTMENT - NIGHT

        SANDY - I'm listening.

        DAVID - I said I love you.

        SANDY - I said I'm listening.

EXTERIOR CITY - DAY

The music plays. Gangster Rap.

The streets are occupied with dope
pushers and dope users.

INTERIOR APARTMENT - DAY

GIT is alongside BOBBY and DAVE
weighing cocaine, then cooking the
cocaine to turn into crack rock. GIT
uses a razor blade to break down the
newly formed crack-rock into small
pieces then places into small bags to
distribute the product out of the trap
(dope hole).

The NARRATOR speaks over the music as
the music volume lowers.

        NARRATOR: DAVE kept his word and
        put me down with BOBBY. BOBBY was
        the father figure in our lives.

HE used to date our MOTHER back in the day, and when they separated some years ago, BOBBY stayed in our lives, and WE respected him as our father. My biological father sold drugs, BOBBY sold drugs, my older brother sold drugs, my uncles and cousins sold drugs, so what are the chances of me not selling drugs.

The music stops.

INTERIOR CAR - EARLY MORNING

GIT gets in the backseat of his MAMA'S car.

> SANDY - Why are you getting in the back seat for? GIT - I'm tired. I haven't slept yet.

> SANDY - Yo ass used to riding in the backseat of the car. Fucking criminal.

> GIT - Laughs. You raised a nigga to be a criminal.

> SANDY - What were you doing up all night? Do you have a curfew?

GIT - The P.O. (probation officer) called DEAN'S house around nine. I checked in. After that, I bucked and hit the streets to get some cash.

SANDY - Then give me some fucking money. Laughing.

GIT - I got you on gas. Damn.

EXTERIOR PRISON VISITATION AREA - DAY

GIT sits on a bench table with his mother waiting for his DAD to come to the area. HE observes the prison's compound. HE watches the INMATES and CORRECTIONAL OFFICERS in the gated fences. GIT has despair in his eyes as HE imagines his future.

GIT sees his DAD walking towards the bench-table. HE stands up.

GIT - Smiles. DADDY-O

DAVID - My nigga. What's up?

DAVID hugs his son and SANDY. They all sit down and talk.

DAVID - Thanks for bringing my lil man.

SANDY - His ass will be in here with you soon.

GIT - Laughs. This lady.

DAVID - This is part of the game son.

GIT - I know.

DAVID - This is the penitentiary my nigga.

GIT - I ain't scared my nigga. I'll handle this shit like a real G.

DAVID - It ain't about handling shit like a G son or fear nigga. It's about being up here in this muthafucker. Captured. Away from life nigga. I've been locked down for eleven with more to do. Do you think my goals in life was to make it to this muthafucker?

GIT nods his head no.

DAVID - Nigga the penitentiary called me, and I fucked up by answering the muthafucking ringer.

SANDY - Ask him what he was doing last night.

DAVID stares at GIT.

DAVID - Let's walk son.

DAVID and GIT get up and walk around the visitation area.

DAVID - You back hustling?

GIT - Yea. I linked up with that nigga DAVE. We are both working for BOBBY now.

DAVID - BOBBY got y'all selling dope?

GIT looks at his dad.

DAVID - Watch DAVE ass. The last time I saw that boy. He ain't looked to right. He on some shit. He took money from your MAMA and all.

GIT - Nah.

DAVID - Hell yeah. She won't lie to me.

GIT - I heard DAVE ass out here gooking (going against the code) and shit.

DAVID - What's your plan? Besides getting money.

GIT - What do you mean?

DAVID - You can't sell dope forever son. You should be working on an exit plan. Have some goals for this shit.

GIT - Laughs.

DAVID - For real. Life ain't no game nigga.

DAVID looks at GIT in the eyes.

DAVID - I had one. My plan was to move y'all from Miami into a house out of town, put your MAMA through school, and drive a waste management truck.

GIT - Yea(smiles). What happened?

DAVID - I had gone to war nigga! I had the crib in Tallahassee dog. Shit was about to be real gravy.

DAVID and GIT stand face to face.

DAVID - My application for the waste management company had gone through. All I had to do was the interview with my sister PEARL'S friend.

GIT - Yea?

DAVID - But the war broke out.

GIT - With them niggaz off seventeenth street?

DAVID - Yea. It takes money to go to war. I handled my business. Put them fuck niggaz down. But I had to get my cash back up, and that's when I got jammed on the road in Duval with twenty-five over my head.

GIT - Damn.

DAVID - Look son. I'm sorry for not being there, but I am not sorry for providing for y'all. The cause at the time was survival and I did what the cause demanded me to do and that's survive.

GIT - I know DAD.

DAVID gave his son a hug, and they walked back to the table. GIT, SANDY, and DAVID continued to talk until the visitation time was over.

INTERIOR CAR - DAY

GIT sits in the front seat of his
MOTHER'S car.

SANDY - Look ANT. I know you are
mad because I left. But I went
through the same bullshit with
your FATHER. Listen to him. He's
been there and done that and look
how HE ended up. You can't sell
dope forever son.

EXTERIOR CAR- DAY

The car backs up and drives off.

SANDY- Now give me some gas
money. Laughs. You going back to
DEAN'S house?

GIT- Nah, take me to GRANNY'S, so
I can check up on her.

INTERIOR CLASSROOM - DAY

GIT is sitting down in the day room at
the juvenile offenders' aftercare
program. There is a male speaker
talking to teenage boys and girls.

NARRATOR: That visit with my DAD
left me in deep thoughts for
days. I accepted the ghetto

reality about my future. I always
thought that my future would be
of me dying from multiple
gunshots wounds or serving a life
sentence in prison. That's all I
have seen in the game, and the
expectations that I had for my
life. GRANNY mentioned to me
about becoming an EMT (Emergency
Medical Technician) and working
on the ambulance. Laughing.
Picture me helping someone.

INTERIOR OFFICE - DAY

GIT is speaking with MS. MIMS, a
guidance counselor at the technical
educational center.

MS. MIMS - Good morning, MR. GRAY

GIT - Smiles. Good morning ma'am.
How are you doing today?

MS. MIMS - I am doing just fine
young man. Just fine.

GIT - Good.

MS. MIMS - How long have you been
out of school?

GIT - For about two years now.

MS. MIMS - Wow! Based on the
results from your TABE (Test of
Adult Basic Education) test. You
haven't missed a beat.

GIT has joy in his face.

GIT - Smiles. Okay.

MS. MIMS - You did very well
overall, MR. GRAY. Especially, in
the math portion.

GIT - I tried. Laughing.

MS. MIMS - You are eligible to
take the GED test when you turn
eighteen.

GIT - I will turn eighteen in
eight months.

MS. MIMS - Good. You can enroll
in the GED PREP classes till
then.

GIT - That's good. Thanks.

GIT stands up and began to walk
towards the door.

MS. MIMS - Young man. What are
your plans after you earn your
GED?

GIT- Enroll at Miami-Dade for the
EMT program. Trying to work on
the ambulance (smiling). You know
what I'm saying.

MS. MIMS- Okay. You must have a
passion for helping others?

GIT- Laughs. I think so. I just
hope that I can get there.

MS. MIMS - I believe that you can
get there. I truly do.

GIT leaves the counselor's office.

EXTERIOR CITY- DAY

GIT walks up the block to the pool
hall.

BOBBY- GIT what it is?

GIT - Chillian.

GIT gives BOBBY a five-hand shake.

BOBBY - I see you on time boy.
You ready to put some work in?

GIT - Smiles. Hell yea.

BOBBY - DAVE upstairs waiting on
you.

GIT walks up the dark pissy stairwell.
BOBBY is sitting outside of the pool
hall with middle to older aged men.

        BOBBY - Look at this hot dog neck
        ass nigga coming up.

The men laugh as GRAPE walks up the
block singing.

        GRAPE - "Singing"

        BOBBY - Nigga what you happy
        about. You must have got some
        pussy. Laughing

        GRAPE - Sucker ass nigga I'm
        married I always get pussy.

        BOBBY - SHHHIIIITTT!

        DOUBLE J - Nigga dick so clean he
        can stick it in a bowl of collard
        greens and come out without shit.

The men laugh.

        GRAPE - Fuck y'all! That shit
        didn't even make muthafucking
        sense.

The men laugh.

        BOBBY - Shit! You fucking, don't
        make sense.

    GRAPE - Sucker ass nigga. What
    the fuck you are worrying about
    my dick for?

    BOBBY - Fuck you!

    GRAPE - Fuck you!

    BOBBY - Yo ol lady done fed the
    shit outta yo ass. Done turned
    you into a real live chair
    breaker. Laughing. Hot dog neck
    ass nigga!

    GRAPE - Fuck you. Why y'all
    fucking with me for?

    BOBBY - Cause nigga we want some
    muthafucking hot dogs!

    GRAPE - Y'all niggaz must want
    something long and brown.

    DOUBLE J - Fuck you hot dog neck
    ass nigga!

The men laugh.

A woman pulls up in a car and beeps
the horn.

    BOBBY - There goes your ol lady
    now.

GRAPE looks back at the car.

BOBBY - (whispers) I bet she got some food for this nigga.

The woman rolls down her window.

BOBBY - Hey MS. GRACE.

The other men wave at the lady in the car.

MS. GRACE - Hey y'all.

MS. GRACE - Come on GRAPE. I had done cooked. Let's go.

BOBBY - (whispers) I told y'all.

GRAPE - I ain't ready to go. I just came up to this muthafucker.

MS. GRACE - GRAPE!

GRAPE -GRACE!

MS. GRACE - Let's go!

GRAPE - I ain't ready to go.

MS. GRACE- Man, get yo hot dog neck ass in this muthafucking car. I got shit to do.

The men laugh. GRAPE walks to the car and get in.

> BOBBY - I'll never get married and turn into a hot dog neck ass nigga.

The men laugh.

EXTERIOR CITY- EVENING

The music plays. Rhythm and blues.

A young woman is walking up the street. Her name is being called by GIT as he jogs to catch up with the young woman. GIT is a block away.

> GIT - LASHAWN! LASHAWN!

The young woman does not turn around.

> GIT - LASHAWN!

GIT runs up to the young woman and hugs her from behind.

> GIT - LASHAWN!

The music stops.

> LASHAWN - Okay ANTHONY. You are calling out my muthafucking government yo.

> GIT - Laughing. Okay PRINCESS.

LASHAWN and GIT kiss.

LASHAWN - Ain't you supposed to
be at work?

GIT - Shit nine (police) hotter
than a muthafucker. They rushed
12th street earlier, and they are
hitting any spot with some
action. So, we closed.

LASHAWN - For real?

GIT - Hell yeah.

LASHAWN - What 'cha bout to get
into?

GIT - You.

LASHAWN - Smiles.

GIT - Wanna go see a movie?

LASHAWN nods her head yes. LASHAWN and
GIT walk down the street towards the
Metro rail.

The music volume lowers as the
NARRATOR speaks.

NARRATOR: I've been in love with
PRINCESS since I was born.
Laughing. The ghetto PRINCESS. So
beautiful with a perfect smile.
She and I have similar
backgrounds. We are children of

the game. Both of our fathers
were incarcerated on dope
charges. Her dad, BIG JOHN opened
the dope spot that I was slanging
at. So, she understood the game
and how I was living.

The music stops.

INTERIOR APARTMENT- AFTERNOON

GIT, DAVE, and BOBBY are in the
apartment selling drugs.

>BOBBY - GIT you are doing good
>boy.

>GIT - Bet.

>BOBBY - When it's your shift. The
>money is neat. You put the ones
>with the ones, the fives with the
>fives, tens with the tens, and
>twenties with the twenties. I
>like that shit dog.

>GIT - Organization makes shit run
>smooth. When you drop off a pack,
>the cash is ready to go.

>BOBBY- Yea I seen that shit. Let
>me ask you something, the count
>been over the last two bags?

GIT - Yea. When they want nics
($5 crack rocks), I break the
quarters ($25 crack rocks) down.
Sometimes I cut forty or forty-
five out. I put the rest as
extra.

DAVE shakes his head no and stares at
GIT.

BOBBY- Yea I saw that shit. I
thought I was tripping. I saw a
rubber band with a paper saying
extra.

GIT - Yea. That's from me.

BOBBY - Nigga it was five hundred
over. Laughing.

GIT - Man, I appreciate the
opportunity B. I don't take
nothing that's ain't mine or owe
to me.

NARRATOR: I learned at a very
young age that if you must lie or
steal from someone, then you must
be afraid of that person. Because
if you are not afraid of anyone,
you will tell them the truth and
take what's theirs with their
knowledge of knowing it.

BOBBY - GIT, I appreciate that. I
tell you what. I'll give you the
five hundred, and next time just
bust down the extra down the
middle with me.

GIT - You sure?

BOBBY - Yea.

BOBBY gives GIT the nod and leaves the
room. GIT and DAVE break down the dope
at the table.

GIT - That nigga B alright.

DAVE - Man, what the fuck you
doing? Telling this nigga that
shit.

GIT - Nigga the shit is extra
bruh.

DAVE - That nigga got plenty of
money. I've been breaking the
bond down since day one.

GIT - Yea?

DAVE - I break them quarters down
at the beginning of my shift.
Sell the extra first. If I don't
sell out, I tell that nigga the
spot is slow.

GIT - Yea?

GIT has a puzzled look on his face.

DAVE - Nigga you are fucking up
my hustle.

GIT - DAVE I'm trying to eat
fool. All that fucking over shit
that's not my vibe bruh. You do
you and I'll keep my mouth
fucking shut. But for me, I'm
going keep doing what I'm doing.

DAVE - And I'm going to stay
playing for keeps.

GIT - Luv.

DAVE - Luv.

GIT gives DAVE a five handshake.

GIT honored the code of being his
brother's keeper. GIT remembers what
his FATHER told him that DAVE was on
some shit, and now HE is seeing it for
HIMSELF.

EXTERIOR AUNT DEAN'S HOUSE- NIGHT

DEAN is sitting on the front porch
talking with TWO WHITE MEN from the
Mormon church. GIT approaches the

porch thinking that the white men were
police officers.

     DEAN - Hey GIT!

     GIT - What's up DEAN?

GIT looks towards the men.

     GIT - Look it's 8:39 and my
     curfew is for nine.

DEAN laughs.

     DEAN - Nah GIT, these men are
     from some kind of church.

     GIT - What the hell y'all doing
     over here?

The two men look puzzled.

     GIT - At this time! Y'all must be
     lost or something?

DEAN shakes her head.

     WHITE MAN #1 - We are from the
     Church of Jesus Christ of Latter-
     day Saints.

     GIT - You are in the church of
     Opa-Locka right now, and yawl
     meet Jesus Christ if yawl fuck
     around in this neighborhood like
     this.

DEAN - GIT!

GIT - Sorry DEAN (laughing), look man I'm saying this isn't a very good neighborhood to be fucked up in. Sir.

DEAN - This boy.

WHITE MAN #1 - We are only here to spread the word of Jesus Christ.

GIT - You crazy as fuck.

DEAN - GIT!

DEAN stands up.

DEAN - Listen I'm not interested in you all religion but talk to this boy. He needs all the help in the world.

GIT - DEAN! Laughing.

DEAN goes back in the house.

WHITE MAN #2 - Are you interested?

GIT - I respect the fact that y'all came thru this mother fucker on bikes and shit like this.

GIT stares at the men up and down with an aggressive look.

GIT - I'm on probation homie, and I got a 9 o'clock curfew. If you slide back thru, I'll fuck with y'all.

The WHITE MEN smile.

WHITE MAN #1 - See you next week.

GIT - Whatever.

EXTERIOR PROJECTS- NIGHT

DAVE approaches a man on the porch. There are several guns around this man.

DAVE - Yo!

FOOL - Who that?

DAVE - Me nigga!

DAVE gives FOOL a five handshake.

DAVE - What's good FOOL?

FOOL - Shit! What the lick read?

DAVE - I got something nigga.

FOOL - Yea!

DAVE - Hell yeah!

FOOL and DAVE sit on the porch.

DAVE - Man, my sucker ass brother
on some bullshit with this nigga
BOBBY. This nigga fucking up my
lil cushion FOOL.

FOOL - At the spot?

DAVE - Yea nigga. GIT talking
about respect and loyalty and
shit. Don't wanna take what's not
his. That nigga gookin (going
against the code). Shit, he needs
to understand that this is the
game. You gotta get it how you
live out chea feel me.

FOOL - That's Bruh doe.

DAVE - He's fucking up.

FOOL - What's on your mind nigga?

DAVE - Robbin the shit.

FOOL laughs.

FOOL - That's Bobby's spot. Ain't
that nigga like daddy and shit.
Laughs. You a muthafucking fool
boy.

DAVE - What they do?

FOOL - Shit, I'm all in. Now, if they buck you know how I get down.

DAVE - Naw. The shit gonna be sweet. I got the key to the spot. We'll hit it on the 1st.

FOOL - Ain't that's a Friday?

DAVE - Hell yeah. That shit should be booming. That nigga B usually keep a whole one and a half in there on the first.

FOOL - Hell fuck yea! This the lick that a nigga been waiting on.

DAVE gives FOOL a five handshake.

EXTERIOR POOL HALL - NIGHT

A group of men are standing outside of the pool hall talking. DAVE and FOOL are watching the spot in a car from a distance. They are dressed in all black. GIT is going up and down the pissy stairwell serving the customers from the apartment.

YOUNG NIGGA - A check dis out dog. I took this broad out the other night dog. She kept going to the muthafucking bathroom. I mean all fucking night. At the lil restaurant she went twice. At the movies, she went before and after.

DOUBLE J - You were counting?

YOUNG NIGGA - Hell yeah! She went so many times that I had to keep a count on her pissy ass.

The men laugh.

YOUNG NIGGA - Let me finish bruh. I dropped her off right. I'm like let me use the bathroom. In my mind, I'm thinking like you went to this muthafucker all night. Enough for the both of us. So, I wanted to see what's so special about her bathroom. Laughing.

DOUBLE J - This silly ass young nigga!

The men laugh.

YOUNG NIGGA - So I slid on the couch with her right. We are kissing and shit. I tried to touch her. She slapped my hand. I

tried again. And she slapped my
hand again. I'm like damn. So, I
popped the fuck off and left
right. Now she is spraying me and
shit calling me crazy.

DOUBLE J - Cause nigga you are
crazy!

YOUNG NIGGA - What 'cha you mean?

DOUBLE J - Crazy nigga. Her
period was on. That's why she
needed to keep going to the
bathroom.

The men laugh.

YOUNG NIGGA - For real?

EXTERIOR CAR - NIGHT

DAVE and FOOL continue to watch from a
distance. They observe GIT going up
and down the stairwell.

DAVE - We should be in there for
at least one minute. We gonna
slide thru the back as soon as
Bruh leaves the door. FOOL, my
nigga hit that bitch quick. Get
the stash and be out.

GIT goes back up the stairs. DAVE and FOOL exit the vehicle and head towards the back of the building.

THE DOPE FIEND - DAVE what's up?

DAVE - Man, get the fuck on!

DAVE and FOOL both put their ski-masks on. GIT leaves the door walking down the stairs. DAVE uses his key, and the men enters the apartment searching for drugs and money. They found the stash. GIT is standing outside the pool hall.

DOPE FIEND #2 - Yo!

GIT walks back-up the stairs to sell drugs to DOPE FIEND #2. DAVE and FOOL were about to exit the apartment, but they heard GIT coming. They turned off the lights and ran into the bathroom. GIT opens the door but noticed that the lights were turned off.

EXTERIOR APARTMENT - NIGHT

GIT - Hold on!

DOPE FIEND #2 - Everything okay?

GIT - I'll be right back.

GIT walks down the stairs, enters the pool hall, and whispers in BOBBY'S ear.

GIT - Something ain't right. The lights off.

BOBBY - The bulbs must of blew.

GIT - Man, something ain't right

BOBBY - Nigga, this is my spot. Nobody ain't fucking with us. Scary ass nigga! Just turn the fucking bathroom light on.

NARRATOR - My intuition was telling me that something wasn't right.

GIT walks up the stairs. Enters the dark apartment. DOPE FIEND #2 waits at the door. GIT walks through the dark living room. He turns on the bathroom light. There were two mask gunmen (DAVE and FOOL) kneeling. GIT is frightening. He quickly attempts to run but is tripped by one of the gunmen.

MASKED GUNMAN #1 (DAVE) - Where's the dope man?

GIT quickly recognizes his brother's
disguise voice.

>   MASKED GUNMAN #1 (DAVE) - Nigga,
>   where is the dope man?

>   MASKED GUNMAN #2 (FOOL) points a
>   pistol to GIT'S head.

>   GIT - Man, I'd know! (Shakes his
>   head no)

MASKED GUNMAN #1 (DAVE) hits GIT in
the face with a gun.

>   MASKED GUNMAN #1 (DAVE) - Nigga,
>   where the dope man at?

GIT says nothing. MASKED GUNMAN #2
(FOOL) hog ties GIT up. DOPE FIEND #2
hears the noise. Runs down the stairs
to tell BOBBY that his son is in
trouble.

>   DOPE FIEND #2 - They got GIT
>   upstairs. Fucking him up.

>   BOBBY - Who?

BOBBY quickly runs outside of the pool
hall. Surrounded by a crowd of people.
BOBBY yells upstairs to the window
overlooking the street to GIT.

>   BOBBY - GIT! GIT!

MASKED GUNMAN #1 (DAVE)is kicking GIT.

    MASKED GUNMAN #2 (FOOL) - Hold
    up, fool. That's bruh.

GIT looks up.

BOBBY is downstairs panicking.

    BOBBY - Where's the young nigga
    at with the fie (gun)?

    DOUBLE J - Fool just rode off.

BOBBY is asking any of the men in the
crowd do they have a gun.

    BOBBY - Who got a pistol?

BOBBY yells back upstairs.

    BOBBY - GIT! GIT!

The MASKED GUNMEN picked GIT up to the
window.

    GIT - Yeah!

    BOBBY - Who in there with you?

    GIT - I'm good B.

    BOBBY - I'm coming up.

    GIT - Stay down there. I'm good.

    MASKED GUNMAN #1 (DAVE) - Tell
    him to come up.

GIT - Fuck you.

BOBBY stays downstairs. MASKED GUNMAN #1 (DAVE) shoves GIT to the floor and the men left the apartment. GIT escapes the apartment through the back by kicking down the boarded-up window. Beaten, ripped shirt, and shoe less. GIT comes down to BOBBY and the crowd.

BOBBY - Oh shit! GIT!

GIT - I'm good nigga. Let me holla at you.

BOBBY has a stunned look on his face.

GIT- That was DAVE ass.

BOBBY - What the fuck you mean?

GIT - Nigga, that was DAVE and his homeboy who did this shit to me.

BOBBY - For real?

GIT - Hell yeah! Imma kill that fuck nigga.

BOBBY has a puzzled look on his face. DAVE and FOOL drove off in the car.

INTERIOR CAR - NIGHT

                    FOOL - Damn, DAVE why you did
          Bruh like that?

                    DAVE - Man, I had to make sure
          that shit looked real.

                    FOOL - That was fucked up. I did
                    a lot of fuck shit in my life.
                    But to touch Bruh like that.
                    That's fucked up. For real. For
                    real.

          The music plays. Gangster Rap.

          The two men drove to the projects.
          They entered an apartment door. Sit at
          a table. They begin to count the money
          and the drugs that they just robbed
          for.

          The music volumes lower.

                    NARRATOR - I should have listened
                    to my intuition. The vibe felt
                    wrong. My soul was troubled. I
                    knew that danger was a light
                    switch away. Instead, I acted on
                    another man's judgment and
                    entered that apartment. Trust my
                    intuition was a lesson that I
                    learned from the robbery.

          EXTERIOR BACKYARD-DAY

GIT is sitting on a crate in the back
yard at his AUNT DEAN'S house putting
bullets into a magazine clip when his
big homie, BIG ANT walks up.

The music stops.

        BIG ANT - GIT.

        GIT- Oh shit, What's good OG?

        BIG ANT- GIT, my nigga!

GIT stands up. BIG ANT gives GIT a
five handshake.

        BIG ANT- You bout to put work in?

        GIT - Hell yeah.

GIT sits back down.

        GIT - That nigga DAVE played.

        BIG ANT- Yeah?

BIG ANT has a puzzled look on his
face.

        BIG ANT - DAVE, yo brother?

        GIT - Yeah. DAVE played and
        robbed the trap last night. HIM
        and some fuck nigga hit us up. I
        got kicked, pistol whipped, and
        hogged tied up OG.

GIT shows BIG ANT the scars and cuts on his body. BIG ANT stares at GIT.

    GIT - So you know the game, OG. I gotta do what I gotta do.

    BIG ANT- I know. I feel you, but that's yo brother.

BIG ANT kneels, put his hand on GIT'S shoulder.

    BIG ANT - Yo brother. I done a lot of shit out here my nigga. I seen a lot of dirty shit out here too but certain shit you gotta let ride and think youngster. THINK! You see the game turns us all dirty. Whether we like it or not. DAVE played on that part. Now you feel that you gotta put work in on your own brother on some G shit. I feel you but GIT!

BIG ANT shakes his head no.

    GIT- Kane and Able OG.

    BIG ANT - That's yo brother nigga. Where were y'all?

    GIT - At BOBBY'S spot.

          BIG ANT - BOBBY? Y'all step
          daddy?

BIG ANT has a puzzled look on his
face.

          GIT - Yeah.

          BIG ANT - BOBBY got y'all selling
          dope?

GIT looks at BIG ANT.

          BIG ANT - What did BOBBY say?

          GIT - He says he will handle it.

          BIG ANT - Let BOBBY handle it.
          BOBBY love y'all too much to kill
          him. Let him handle it.

          GIT - Fuck that!

Song starts to play at a low volume.
Gangster Rap.

          BIG ANT - GIT. I need a favor.

          GIT - OG. I gotta kill him.

          BIG ANT - GIT you gotta let this
          one go baby. For me. You are not
          soft if you let this slide. It
          shows that you got a good heart
          on not killing your own brother
          after he snaked you. Life lesson

young nigga. Stay the fuck away
from snakes.

BIG ANT gives GIT a hug.

    BIG ANT - On the set (section)
GIT. Let this one go.

    GIT - I got you OG.

Music volumes increases.

EXTERIOR NIGHT

GIT is sitting on the front porch at
AUNT DEAN'S House reading bible verses
with the TWO WHITE MEN from the Mormon
church.

BOBBY beats on DAVE and DAVE leaves
MIAMI.

The music stops.

    NARRATOR: After being robbed by
    my brother, I thought long and
    hard about my future in the game.
    If it wasn't for the big homie, I
    would have had killed my brother
    for during some snake shit. My
    brother. Damn, me and this nigga
    got the same mother and father.
    He's my older brother. I did not
    see that coming from DAVE ass.

After the robbery, I continued my life in the drug game. I just moved with more precaution. I always kept a gun on me after that incident. I made a promise to myself that I'll never be a victim again. Life goes on. I completed the four months that I had on probation and continue to pursue the goal of earning a GED. Here it is. I am studying for my GED during the daytime, selling dope at night, and GOD is starting to come look for me.

GIT gets on his knees and pray.

GIT - Dear GOD O Heavenly FATHER I pray for my wrong doings, understand that I am a child criminal minded living foolish, bless me to see no more cases and I'll walk in righteous steps, a covenant that I'll never break, and you can put that on my death.

ACT OF CARING

The caring acts for GIT (GANGSTA IN TRAINING) began as a teenage drug dealer recognizing that THE MAN with a known substance abuse history was requesting to buy drugs was in heart failure. GIT displayed the generalized key values in caring for another individual that he decided not to sell THE MAN drugs because he understood that THE MAN was experiencing an unstable medical problem and that crack-cocaine would have had worsen THE MAN'S condition to death. GIT'S act of caring was a blessing to a stranger in a troubled environment. The information for GIT recognizing that he has the potential to become someone in life came from the verbal statements of THE MAN and GRANNY. THE MAN implied that GIT was meant to be more than a drug-dealer and GRANNY provided GIT with the encouragement by stating that he is very smart, he has a good heart, and GOD has something for him to do. The statements were validated by the TABE test results, his commitment to change by continuing to go to school and GIT'S dedication in seeking a higher power to assist in the transition of change. The experiences in the drug game shaped GIT into trusting his intuition, and to apply the standard ethical principles of honesty and integrity to gain the respect of others as shown in his conversation with BOBBY on not taking what isn't HIS.

EXAMINING

"IF YOU DECIDE NOT TO SELL DRUGS, THEN I WOULD HAVE NO ONE TO BUY DRUGS FROM."

- BLIND

INTERIOR CLASSROOM - DAY

GIT is taking the GED test.

NARRATOR: I finally made it to my eighteenth birthday alive and free. Alive and free is a blessing at the age of eighteen in the dope game. I was finally eligible to take the GED test. My MOTHER obtained her GED from Miami Job Corps Center at the age of 23, and my FATHER obtained his from Florida Department of Corrections at the age of 33. I

was able to pass the GED test on
my first attempt. That became a
proud moment for me in my life. I
guess jailhouse thinking can be
the same as freedom actions. I
did not have any run ins with the
laws during the eight months of
GED preparation of selling crack-
cocaine, and of being involved in
a few shootouts. I guess that I'm
lucky or is it that GOD is
looking out for me.

EXTERIOR APARTMENT BUILDING - NIGHT

ZAY TWO is sitting on the steps
smoking a joint when GIT walks up to
him.

> GIT - ZAY!

> ZAY TWO - GIT HOUND, my nigga,
> what they do?

> GIT - BAM!

GIT shows ZAY TWO his high school
diploma.

> ZAY TWO - What the fuck?

ZAY TWO reads it and smiles.

ZAY TWO - Hell yeah, my nigga. I always knew you were a smart nigga.

ZAY TWO gives GIT a five handshake.

ZAY TWO - Hit this. Let's celebrate.

ZAY TWO attempts to pass GIT the joint.

GIT - Nah DEUCE, that ain't for me dog.

ZAY TWO has a puzzled look on his face.

GIT - Celebrate for what? That diploma doesn't mean shit ZAY, if a nigga gonna stay thuging out here.

ZAY TWO - Yeah.

GIT - A nigga just touched 18 fool. Now you know what that means.

ZAY TWO - Penitentiary bound.

GIT - I don't want to be a smart nigga that graduated to the chain gang. You feel me.

          ZAY TWO - What the fuck you gonna
          do?

GIT pauses and firmly stares at ZAY
TWO.

          GIT - Work on the ambulance.

ZAY TWO looks up at GIT and starts
laughing.

          ZAY TWO - Ain't nobody gonna let
          your criminal ass work on no
          ambulance.

          GIT - All my charges are as a
          minor. You see they only do local
          background checks as an adult.
          Nigga I just turned 18, and I
          ain't trying to catch another
          case fool. ZAY, I live in fear of
          a felony dog.

ZAY TWO Laughs.

          GIT - You think it's a game?

          ZAY TWO - What about the dope
          game? GIT you a hustler. Always
          bout a dollar. Why the fuck you
          think we call your ass Scrooge
          for? I still owe you bread from
          the last pack you gave me.

GIT - ZAY fuck the dope game. I
don't want to be a victim of a
plot that was designed for us to
fail.

ZAY TWO folds his arms.

GIT - Shit, we got neutralized
with dope in the seventies and
eighties.

GIT looks up at the sky.

GIT - Shit, PAC was right.

ZAY TWO nods his head yes.

GIT looks at ZAY TWO in the eyes.

GIT - ZAY, rather you a dope
pusher or a dope user you gonna
get fucked by the game.

GIT pauses.

GIT - How many niggaz you know
made it pass 25 alive and free?

ZAY TWO unfolds his arms.

ZAY TWO - Not too many.

GIT - I'm talking legends fool.
Niggaz who made a whole lot of
fucking money and fail before
they were 25. Imagine having a

life sentence over your head
before your 25th birthday or dead
in a fucking coffin. All the
money in the world can't amount
to that bruh.

ZAY TWO - Shit, gotta play by the
rules. The rules say don't get
caught or get caught slipping.

GIT - Nigga you gonna get caught.
These folks see a nigga standing
in the same hole all fucking day
with junkies coming in and out
the mother fucker. You think they
ain't gonna rush the spot?

ZAY TWO - HOUND you are tripping.

GIT - ZAY you are tripping. You
better get on something solid my
nigga. Fuck around and life will
pass you by.

The music plays. Gangster Rap.

GIT gives ZAY TWO a five handshake.

GIT - You can keep that bread
homeboy.

The music lowers as the NARRATOR
speaks.

NARRATOR: ZAY TWO is my outlaw
blood brother from the Leaf. We
had bonded through the system and
the drug game.

The music stops.

INTERIOR APARTMENT - DAY

GRANNY is starring at GIT.

GIT - What's good GRANNY? I know
I look good, but you don't have
to stare at me like that.

GRANNY - Nigga you look like me.
You should be grateful to have my
genes. When I was in my twenties
as a nurse, living in New York
City I had a body shaped like a
Coke-Cola bottle. Got damn!

GIT - Now you just shaped like
the can. Laughing.

GRANNY gives GIT that look.

GRANNY - I was looking at you
because I am picturing that EMT
uniform on you.

GIT has a look of disbelief on his
face.

GRANNY - Did you enroll at Miami-Dade yet?

GIT - Not yet. GRANNY do you think that I am college material?

GRANNY nods her head yes.

NARRATOR: GRANNY was on a fixed income. The money she received was barely enough to support her. It was a struggle for us, but she never asked me how I was getting things like new clothes and shoes. I guess she didn't want to know the truth.

GIT - GRANNY I don't think my kind is made for college.

GRANNY - What is your kind?

GIT - GRANNY I am made in these streets. I come from a teenage mother and a daddy as a convict. I have been in and out system since I was 12 years old. Abandoned by my MOTHER, robbed by my BROTHER, and living with my FATHER'S curse. What my kind can offer a college?

GRANNY has watery eyes.

GIT - I thought about joining the
Army and becoming an EMT through
that route.

GRANNY - Come sit next to me
ANTHONY. Come here.

GIT sits next to GRANNY.

GRANNY - I was born in 1926. You
have no idea what my kind has
experienced in this country. I
was not allowed to go to college
down here. I had to go way to
Kentucky to attend school. My
kind was beaten, raped, lynched,
and jailed just for standing up
for the decency right to be
treated as human beings. My kind
your kind are Negroes. Meaning
that every knee should grow.
Every generation should be better
than the last generation.

GRANNY hugs GIT.

The music plays. Soulful Gospel.

GRANNY - Enroll in college and
you will see what our kind can
do.

GIT leaves GRANNY'S house and walking
towards the Metrorail.

GRANNY is on her knees praying.

The music volume lowers as the NARRATOR speaks.

> NARRATOR: GRANNY was right. The history of black folks in America has not been a pretty one. We were kidnapped, chained and enslaved for centuries. After that was over, we became genetically battered from psychological trauma that caused a loss of cohesiveness in self-value, and we still were able to survive Jim Crow Laws that the Negro should not have a weak gene left. We can overcome any obstacle with the right willpower.

The music stops.

INTERIOR APARTMENT - NIGHT

GIT and ROC are standing at a table counting money. BOBBY had got locked up a couple months later after the incident with DAVE on a probation violation.

> NARRATOR: ROC was running the spot for a while during BOBBY'S

incarceration in the county on a 364 (364 days in the County Jail). I already had it in my mind that I was going to quit this shit. ME and ROC had a few altercations over my decisions not to sell dope to pregnant women, and to JUNKIE RED. One time, JUNKIE RED gave me a bloody five-dollar bill that HE said that HE got from snatching a book (purse). When I saw the blood on the five-dollar bill, I pictured a beaten woman who just had her pocketbook taken.

ROC - Damn GIT, shit runs smooth when you are working. The place is vacuumed and cleaned. Every stack is rubber-banded up in a brown paper bag.

GIT - ROC you know we can catch a case off the residue. I feel like if I keep the table, stove, and floor cleaned them crackers (the system) can't find shit after the work is flushed.

ROC - Tight-work GIT. Not the same for ANDRE pussy ass. This nigga just throws the money in

the bag. This nigga be having
dope everywhere. This nigga
better tighten up. I might
promote your ass to LT
(lieutenant) GIT.

GIT and ROC laughs.

GIT - ROC I wanted to holla at
you, my nigga.

ROC - What's up?

GIT - You know a nigga was
studying for the GED test, right?

ROC - I know.

GIT - I passed bruh.

ROC smiles. Gives GIT a five
handshake.

ROC - Good shit young nigga.

GIT - I'm thinking about leaving
my nigga.

ROC - What you going out of town
or something? You need a few days
off?

GIT - Nah bruh, thinking about
leaving the game.

ROC stares at GIT.

ROC - And do what?

GIT - Go to college and become an
EMT to work on the ambulance.

ROC laughs.

ROC - College? Nigga you a
hustler. College ain't for you
nigga.

ROC and GIT continue to count money.

GIT - What do you mean?

ROC laughs at GIT.

ROC - A matter of fact I'm going
to promote your ass to LT dog.

GIT - ROC I'm leaving the game
dog.

ROC takes out his gun and taps it on
the table. ROC has a serious look on
his face.

ROC - GIT ain't no getting out.
The only way out is the grave or
the jailhouse.

GIT looks at ROC.

The music plays. Gangster Rap.

ROC - You a good hustler! And you
ain't scared to slang iron (shoot
a gun) my nigga. What the fuck
you wanna go to college for and
work on some punk ass ambulance
truck?

GIT has a disbelief look on his face.

ROC - Stick with me lil homie I
got a few more spots that I can
let you run, and I got plans to
take all this shit over.

GIT - ROC you don't feel me dog.
My old boy (father) doing 25 and
my step old boy, BOBBY, is locked
the fuck up now. I got a chance
my nigga to do something
different.

ROC looks at his gun then put it on
the table.

ROC - GIT if you walk out the
door ain't no coming back college
boy.

GIT starts to walk towards the door
then turns around at ROC.

GIT - Check the count it should
be over.

GIT exit out the door.

ROC continues to count the money.

The music stops.

>ROC- College? (shakes his head no)

INTERIOR DEPARTMENT STORE CAFE -DAY

GIT is sitting at a restaurant table inside a department store at the cafe with his mother filling out a job application for an overnight warehouse position.

>NARRATOR: The dope game is a dirty game. I was fortunate enough to have the mind set on not getting caught in the hype of the game. I witnessed too many of my family members and homeboys inherit the rewards of the game through penitentiary time, bullets, bullshit, and psychological scars that can never be healed. I left the game as a man. I never snitched on anybody, didn't owe anybody shit, and my face was clean in DADE COUNTY.

My AUNTIE DEAN'S house had become a place that was not right for me to live, so I gave my MAMA some money to let me stay on her couch until I could figure things out.

GIT and SANDY are approached by a Jamaican Manager of the cafe, SHARON BLAIR.

>MS. SHARON - Good morning.

>GIT - Good morning, ma'am.

SANDY acknowledges the woman with a smile.

>MS. SHARON - Oh, me see the boy is very polite.

GIT has a big smile on his face.

>MS. SHARON - What position are you applying for young man?

>GIT - The overnight warehouse position ma'am.

>MS. SHARON - You like working nights?

>GIT - I have no preference now. I am just looking for a job ma'am. I'll take anything.

MS. SHARON - Oh, me see the boy
is very honest you hear.

SANDY has a surprise look on her face.

MS. SHARON - Are you in school?

GIT - I start college in two
months.

MS. SHARON - What you will be
going to college for?

GIT - I will be taking
prerequisites to enter the EMT
program to work on the ambulance
in another year.

MS. SHARON - Oh, me see the boy
has goals.

GIT - Yes ma'am (Smiles).

SANDY has a big surprise look on her
face.

MS. SHARON - I tell you what.
Finish the application and give
it to me. Are you able to do a
drug test today?

GIT - Yes ma'am (Smile).

GIT glad that he had given up smoking
marijuana months ago. If HE did not

quit, this opportunity would have had passed him by.

SANDY looks puzzled. GIT gives the application to SHARON BLAIR and completed the urine drug screening.

> NARRATOR: Just like that I had a job. It was a relief. I was filling out application after application, and it was becoming frustrating. At first, I was worried about my juvenile criminal record, but the applications specify have you been arrested as an adult, and my answer to the question was no. Laughs.

INTERIOR CAR - DAY

SANDY and GIT are riding in the car together.

> SANDY - What was that bull shit back there?

> GIT - What you mean?

> SANDY - That college talk.

> GIT - I told you I enrolled in school a month after I got my GED. I'm just waiting for the

next semester to start in a
couple of months.

SANDY – What are you going to
school for?

GIT – MA, you don't listen to
shit that I say. I'm going to be
an EMT.

SANDY looks at GIT.

SANDY – Nigga you a criminal.

GIT has a serious look on his face.

GIT – MA, I am not a criminal. I
am a product of my environment.
You just don't know what's in my
head.

SANDY looks at GIT.

GIT – I still have visions in my
head from when I was six years
old, and I seen a nigga get shot.
That shit ain't normal.

GIT expresses anger on his face.

GIT – You raised a nigga this
way. Since I was a lil boy you
put it in my head that I was
never going to be shit in life
but an inmate.

SANDY - Because you were bad.

GIT - How?

SANDY - How many times have your
teachers called me from your
school? How many times have you
got suspended? How many times
your ass got arrested? How many
times ANT? How many muthafuckin
times boy?

GIT shakes his head yes.

SANDY - You just don't understand
how bad you were. That's why I
left your ass.

GIT - MA, when I was in the
second grade, and they tested me
to be gifted. They told you to
move me to advance classes.

GIT looks at SANDY with tears in his
eyes.

GIT - The school told you that. I
remember that. You didn't.
Imagine being a kid in class that
finished the work first way ahead
of the other kids then having
nothing to do, so I was
disruptive which led to you being
called by the school.

GIT pauses.

> GIT - When I was 10 years old, I
> remember showing you a package
> from the school about a college
> savings plan and that I wanted to
> go to college to be a
> meteorologist when I grow up.

SANDY laughs.

> SANDY - I remember.

> GIT - You told me that I ain't
> going to no college that I was
> going to prison to be with my
> DADDY.

GIT wipes the tears off his face.

> GIT - I'm glad that I never
> listened to you. Now, I'm not
> focusing on doing time in a
> correctional institution I'm
> trying to do time in an
> educational institution.

The music plays. Gangster Rap.

GIT has a serious look on his face.

EXTERIOR COLLEGE CAMPUS - DAY

GIT is walking around Miami-Dade College North Campus with a smile from ear to ear.

The music volume lowers as the NARRATOR speaks.

> NARRATOR: I was released from jail on November 6, 2001, and now I am starting college on January 7, 2003. In 14 months, I was able to overcome the obstacles in the drug game and gun violence to develop characteristic traits in leadership, integrity, compassion, respectfulness, and honesty.

GIT sits in the front of the class. Very attentive to the professor and participating in all the classroom discussions.

> NARRATOR: My testimony is that GOD shifted me from a jail cell to a chair in a college classroom. Now, I know that jailhouse thinking can be the same as freedom actions.

ANTHONY goes to the corner of the library to pray on his knees.

The music stops.

>ANTHONY - I am one in a million
>standing tall, succeeding against
>the grain with my back against
>the wall, blessed to have a
>warrior's heart, to conquer
>life's challenging missions,
>self-discipline, third eye-open
>to see success as my only vision.

EXAMINING

The caring process for ANTHONY
continues as HE is transitioning from
GIT (GANGSTA IN TRAINING). ANTHONY is
maturing into a young college student
from a teenage drug-dealer. ANTHONY
makes the mature decision by moving in
with HIS MOTHER to figure things out
and to find HIMSELF searching for a
higher power rather than the bullets
that await for HIM in the street life.
At a very young age, ANTHONY
challenged HIMSELF to go against the
grain and to leave the drug game.
ANTHONY lost social support from HIS
peers, but through the mentorship and
love from GRANNY, ANTHONY was able to
gain the courage to obtain self-

achievement by earning HIS GED,
enrolling in college, getting a job,
and developing a new outlook on life.
In examining ANTHONY'S decisions,
ANTHONY has begun to focus on a
greater purpose in life than to be an
inmate like HIS FATHER. ANTHONY'S up
bringing from a child with untreated
post-traumatic stress disorder caused
by witnessing a man getting shot at
the age of six years old to HIMSELF
living by the code of gun violence
lowered his self-worth but motivated
by HIS realization that GOD guided HIM
from a jail cell to college. Allowed
ANTHONY to understand the demand of
self-recognition in depicting that he
can be the one from an unfortunate
environment that can succeed against
the odds.

THE FORMULATION

"If there is no struggle, there is no
progress."

- Frederick Douglass

INTERIOR COUCH — MORNING

ANTHONY is on his MOTHER'S couch sleeping. HE is in a deep sleep. Dreaming of the shooting that HE witnessed as a young boy.

EXTERIOR STREET CORNER IN OVERTOWN — DAY

LITTLE ANTHONY and LITTLE DAVE are playing in the dirt as they are observing three MEN arguing. MAN #1 is on an Electric Scooter Moped. MAN #2 has a gun and is asking MAN #3 where is his money? MAN #2 shoots MAN #3 in both of his legs. MAN #3 falls on his back and begs for his life. As MAN #3 begs for his life, he turns and looks at LITTLE ANTHONY and asked the little boy for help before being shot in the head by MAN #2.

INTERIOR COUCH — MORNING

The sound of a single gunshot wakes ANTHONY up in sweat. HE gets up and gets ready for school.

> NARRATOR: My life is heading in the right direction now. My mind is only thinking about school, work, and helping my family

particularly my sister TOYA and
her baby AALIYAH. I am living at
both my MAMA'S place and GRANNY'S
place. Like my childhood. They
only have room for me to sleep on
their couches. A couch beats a
jail cell any day. The job at the
cafe and the money that I had
saved up kept me focused on
figuring things out. MY MAMA'S
spot was closer to the job, and
GRANNY'S place was closer to the
school. For the first time in my
life, I felt normal. I can't
believe that I am in college and
living the right way. I lost
contact with the TWO WHITE MEN
from the Mormon Church JACOB and
SETH. PRINCESS and I relationship
had faded away. BOBBY was still
locked up in the county, and I
heard that DAVE pussy ass was
back in Miami, living with some
woman in the Pork and Beans
projects. Every day I still think
about killing that nigga.

ANTHONY is singing a prayer.

ANTHONY - 'GOD bless the real,
kill all the phony, GOD bless the

real, free all my homies, the day
I'm at peace, is when my brother
is six feet deep, GOD bless the
real.'

INTERIOR CLASSROOM – DAY

ANTHONY is sitting in the classroom
with other students listening to the
professor speak.

PROFESSOR BUKHARI – When
discussing under privilege in
America, a born citizen of this
country cannot say they go
without.

STUDENT ONE (MALE) – What do you
mean?

PROFESSOR BUKHARI – There are no
poor people in America.

STUDENT TWO (FEMALE) – That is an
untrue statement.

PROFESSOR BUKHARI – Why?

STUDENT TWO (FEMALE) – Plenty of
people in the ghettos of America
would argue that life for them is
rough. The class agrees. ANTHONY
sits up in his seat.

> PROFESSOR BUKHARI - Please
> explain.

> STUDENT TWO (FEMALE) - Take a
> neighborhood like Overtown. The
> crime rate is very high over
> there, people can barely pay
> their rent, and they have a
> really bad drug problem.

ANTHONY looks at his Outlaw tattoo on
his right forearm and covers it with
his left hand.

> PROFESSOR BUKHARI - Have you ever
> been to Overtown?

> STUDENT TWO (FEMALE) - No. I'm
> afraid that I might get shot.
> Laughs.

The class laughs. ANTHONY remains
silent. But HE is very attentive.

> PROFESSOR BUKHARI - Well, I have
> driven there on a few occasions.

> STUDENT TWO (FEMALE) - Did you
> get shot? Laughs.

The class laughs.

> PROFESSOR BUKHARI - No I did not
> get shot. I admit that the way

that the community is portrayed in the news may seem scary.

STUDENT ONE (MALE) - More like tales from the hood scary.

The class laughs. ANTHONY looks at his classmates with anger.

PROFESSOR BUKHARI - I observed a community no different than any other community. There were churches there, schools, parents walking with their kids, stores, and people living their everyday lives. But what stood out to me the most. There were several fancy cars with big shinny rims that my husband loved, and I saw teenage boys with sneakers that looked like they cost over a hundred dollars a pair. That community did not look very poor to me compared to the slums of third world countries.

STUDENT ONE (MALE) - The boys probably were drug-dealers.

ANTHONY thinks to himself that HE was a teenage boy that was standing on the corner selling drugs in some fresh pair of Js.

STUDENT TWO (FEMALE) - Drug
dealers are the worst kind of
people. They poisoned their own
communities. Shoot people who try
to invade their turf. My
grandfather was a prosecutor and
told me that they should be
locked up forever. They are
monsters.

PROFESSOR BUKHARI - How come the
poorest communities in America
have the worst drug problems?

The class remains silence.

PROFESSOR BUKHARI looks at STUDENT TWO
(FEMALE).

PROFESSOR BUKHARI - In your
community, are there random drug
transactions taking place on
multiple corners?

STUDENT TWO (FEMALE) shakes her head
no.

PROFESSOR BUKHARI - You spoke
earlier that Overtown has a
really bad drug problem and that
you may get shot by riding
through there, but cannot answer
the question on how come the

poorest communities in America
have the worst drug problems?
Their communities seemed to be
flooded with dealers and addicts,
and yet the labeling of a drug-
dealer is depicted in society's
lenses that sees a teenage boy
standing on the corner as a
monster that should be locked
forever. Instead of seeing a
teenage boy as a child who
inherit the drug trade from his
father or a male role model that
sold drugs. And if provided an
opportunity that teenage boy may
have a caring soul that could
change the world.

PROFESSOR BUKHARI looks at ANTHONY.
ANTHONY smiles.

The music plays. Urban Contemporary
Gospel.

ANTHONY has taken on the role as a
college student very well. HE attends
class regularly and studies in the
school library. HIS good grades have
earned HIM to be on the Academic
Dean's list. HE loves his job at the
cafe making pizza, cleaning tables,
socializing with his coworkers, and

the feeling of being a normal eighteen-year-old. To ANTHONY the feeling of being normal, and not an inmate or criminal is the best feeling in the world.

The music stops.

INTERIOR TESTING CENTER - DAY

> ANNOUNCER - ANTHONY GRAY! ANTHONY GRAY!

> ANTHONY - Yes sir.

The ANNOUNCER hands ANTHONY a sheet of paper with the results.

> ANNOUNCER - Better luck next time kid.

ANTHONY is looking at the paper.

> MIKE - MING YANG, did you pass?

> MING YANG - Shit yea bro I passed.

> MIKE - Yo ANTHONY, did you pass?

> ANTHONY - I missed it by one point.

ANTHONY has a serious look on HIS face.

> MING YANG – Damn bro. You know that you can take it again, next month. Good luck and I am here if you need anything.

ANTHONY nods HIS head yes. MING YANG gives ANTHONY a five handshake.

> NARRATOR – I failed the EMT exam for the State of Florida. Damn! My feelings on the failure were vague. Thinking about ZAY TWO'S comment "don't nobody want your criminal ass working on somebody's ambulance truck."

EXTERIOR MLK METRO RAIL STATION LIBERTY CITY – AFTERNOON

ANTHONY is walking around the station reading quotes by Dr. King for inspiration. ANTHONY is in deep thought on how HE plans on doing better the next time, and ANTHONY is contemplating on rather or not HE is meant for success.

ANTHONY walks down the street to GRANNY'S house.

INTERIOR GRANNY'S HOUSE – AFTERNOON

> GRANNY – How is my EMT?

ANTHONY - GRANNY I failed?

GRANNY - Stop joking around ANT!

ANTHONY gives GRANNY the testing sheet
results. GRANNY reads the paper.

GRANNY - You missed it by one
point.

ANTHONY - Yea.

GRANNY - You just got to study
harder next time baby.

ANTHONY - GRANNY I'm going back
to selling dope!

GRANNY - Nigga you crazy.

ANTHONY starts laughing.

ANTHONY - I'm serious!

GRANNY - Get away from me with
that nigger talk.

ANTHONY - Laughing. All you say
is nigga.

GRANNY - ANTHONY you know why I
say nigga all the time.

ANTHONY - Nah GRANNY.

GRANNY - Because when America
calls me one, I'll be ready.

ANTHONY - What do you mean
GRANNY?

GRANNY - My grandmother taught me
the two of us.

GRANNY walks to her bedroom and goes
in her drawer. She comes back to the
living room with a folded sheet of
paper. GRANNY looks at ANTHONY with
pride in her eyes.

GRANNY - The two of us are who we
are in America. The first thing
you must learn is that we are
human beings that are created by
GOD'S love. ANTHONY read this.

GRANNY hands ANTHONY her birth
certificate. ANTHONY reads the paper.

GRANNY - What is my race?

ANTHONY - Colored.

GRANNY - Who the fuck is colored?
And colored to who?

GRANNY grabs ANTHONY hand tightly. HER
voice becomes aflame.

GRANNY - WE were kidnapped,
chained, enslaved and treated
worse than field animals for

centuries. This country profited off our backs and gave us the first one of us, a NIGGER!

GRANNY has tears in her eyes.

GRANNY - A nigger that is not fully a human being that is mixed with an animal. Ignorant! That nigger. I call myself a nigger every day because I never want to forget how America sees me and what America think of me, so when America calls me one, I will be ready and not react by showing them THEIR nigger.

GRANNY winks her eye at ANTHONY.

GRANNY - Instead I will show them the second one of us, a BAD NIGGA. A bad nigga is an educated person that has knowledge of self and of the world. A bad nigga takes pride in his/her appearance. A bad nigga speaks, walks, and shines with GOD'S grace. A bad nigga that if you touch you will die.

GRANNY gives ANTHONY dap.

GRANNY - Now, show me which one are you!

EXTERIOR PRISON VISITATION AREA - DAY

DAVID is walking towards the picnic table with a smile from ear to ear showing all his gold teeth.

DAVID - Excuse me officer.

DAVID addresses the visitation area.

DAVID - Listen up everybody. If anybody has a heart attack or any other medical issues, please get my son. He just passed the EMT exam.

The inmates, visitors and officers cheer and clap for ANTHONY.

DAVID gives ANTHONY a big hug.

DAVID - I'm proud of you champ. You stuck with it. You missed the first one by a point. You didn't give up and passed the second one with flying colors.

DAVID gives ANTHONY a five handshake.

DAVID - My nigga. Bad nigga.

ANTHONY smiles.

The inmates come over to the table to congratulate ANTHONY.

> INMATE #1 - Change the game on them. Fuck this shit in here.

> INMATE #2 - This ain't where is at homeboy.

> DAVID - I told him.

> INMATE #3 - Stay rocking them Js.

ANTHONY laughs.

DAVID and ANTHONY walk around the visitation area.

> DAVID - How's school going?

> ANTHONY - Shit going straight. I had to straighten a mark at the college house though.

> DAVID - Yea! What happened?

> ANTHONY - This duck ass nigga asked me for 50 cents. I shot it to him. A couple days later the nigga asked me for a dollar. Bamn. I shot it to him.

DAVID folds his arms.

> ANTHONY - DAD I walk around with 500 or better daily. I'm thinking

that fool is a struggling college
student, so I had no pressure
shooting him change. I heard him
in class saying I bet that nigga
in them Js give me money. Then a
few seconds later he asked me for
a dollar. I told him to get it in
blood. Then, I caught his ass
solo. Walked up to the mark.
Showed him some bread (money) and
told him to take it. I told the
pussy nigga who I am and what I
stand for. His bitch ass folded.
I made sure I got that sucker ass
change back too.

DAVID has a serious look on his face.

DAVID - You did what you supposed
to do.

DAVID gives ANTHONY a five handshake.

DAVID - If buddy would have
played in here like that, it
would have been no talking.

ANTHONY nods his head yes.

DAVID - But you ain't in here
(aggressive voice). The G code
that you learned in the game
don't apply in a mark's world. If

buddy would have bucked, what would you did?

ANTHONY - Fucked his ass up.

DAVID - ANTHONY don't let a mark throw you off of your G. Stand on your pivot firmly. You must realize that your ghetto tactics would land you in prison. You have to learn to adapt to the outside world and survive to your advantage. Use your ghetto tactics to your advantage only. Busters come a thousand times. Nigga you know for every real nigga there are a thousand busters. Stay buster free, ANTHONY.

Music plays. Gangster Rap.

The visit is over. ANTHONY and DAVID say their goodbyes.

INTERIOR PRISON - NIGHT

An inmate is getting stabbed by another inmate in a blind spot. Three inmates are raping another inmate inside the prison's church. DAVID is doing push-ups in the jail cell while

his cell mate sharpens his shank
(prison made knife).

The music stops.

    CELLMATE - What's on your mind
KILLA?

    DAVID - My son.

    CELLMATE - The EMT?

    DAVID - Yeah! He had to
straighten a mark at the college
house.

    CELLMATE - Damn. Tell him it's
always gonna be a mark in this
world. He gotta stay the fuck
away from them before he ends up
in here.

    DAVID - I told him.

    CELLMATE - Shit I wish that I
would have walked away from them
sucker ass niggaz that I killed.
I killed both of their pussy
asses. Now, I'm going to die in
this shit.

CELLMATE looks at the knife.

    CELLMATE - Fuck it. The G code.
Commit murder or die.

DAVID stops during push-ups and gives
CELLMATE dap.

    DAVID - The G code.

DAVID resumes doing push-ups.

    DAVID - I just hope that my lil
    man can figure things out
    differently. I just hope that GOD
    put his hands on him and guide
    him through.

    CELLMATE - Shit he gave up
    selling dope. GOD has to be in
    the mix somewhere. Not too many
    young niggaz quit to take a job
    at a pizza spot.

INTERIOR LIBRARY - NIGHT

ANTHONY goes to a corner to pray.

INTERIOR PRISON CELL - NIGHT

    CELLMATE - Let's get this bitch
    lit.

CELLMATE bangs on the bunk to a make a
beat.

    CELLMATE - Sound off KILLA.

DAVID stops doing push-ups, stands up
and starts to rap.

DAVID - Bloods being shed, and nobody is crying, LORD is like an epidemic steady multiplying, and these snakes still got us going against the grain, the breed of souljaz calling on you LORD feel our pain.

INTERIOR LIBRARY - NIGHT

ANTHONY is on his knees praying.

INTERIOR PRISON CELL - NIGHT

DAVID - Cause on earth ain't no answer to the question why, tattoos on our bodies stressing how we'll die, in these streets it's a war between soft and hard, and I seen too many killed to ever drop my guard, one thing for sure in this game we all started nerdy, but for the love of money now we all dirty, handle the jury for me LORD and I won't forget, to stress GOD to a thug every time I spit, and to the brothers in the joint I'll always shout, to stress the pain in your hearts till they take me out, since the rules to the game ain't being rehearsed, the breed of souljaz

in this crooked land we bomb
first.

THE FORMULATION

The caring process for ANTHONY GRAY
continues with ANTHONY formulating
specific goals and outcomes that are
measurable, meaningful, and realistic.
In just two years since HIS release,
ANTHONY has earned a GED and has
become an EMT. In accomplishing these
goals, ANTHONY actions attained the
philosophy of jailhouse thinking can
be the same as freedom actions. In the
setting of higher learning, ANTHONY
has learned the pros and cons of
society's views on the ghetto from the
classroom discussion. This brought new
insight to HIM on the culture that HE
represents. With the supportive
involvement of his FATHER from behind
bars and HIS elderly GRANDMOTHER,
ANTHONY has become inspired to
continue to focus on a higher
education, and not to resort to
violence as a means of problem
solving.

PERFORMANCE

"You went from a thug to a nerd."

- Big Homie Dre Dawg

Music plays. Rap.

INTERIOR STRIP CLUB - NIGHT

ANTHONY is alongside BOBBY, ROC, and
DRE DAWG at a local strip club in
MIAMI enjoying the night life.

ANTHONY'S timeline:

☐ Released from Southern Glades
Youth Camp, November of 2001.

☐ Earned a General Educational
Diploma from Lindsey Hopkins
Technical Educational Center,
September of 2002.

☐ Became an Emergency Medical
Technician in the State of
Florida, October of 2003.

☐ Earned an Associate in Arts Degree from Miami-Dade College, April of 2005.

☐ Now enrolled at Nova Southeastern University in the School of Nursing, August of 2006.

The music volume lowers as the NARRATOR speaks.

NARRATOR: I put in different types of work over the last 5 years. I studied hard and stayed focused on working and school. I met some encouraging people along the way. Willie Williams the First Responder Instructor. Ms. Romanila Oliver a guidance counselor in the EMS (Emergency Medical Services) program at Miami-Dade College Medical Campus. Mr. Dorian L. Bennett, a counselor with the workforce program sponsored by the City of Miami.

The music stops.

NARRATOR: Since my childhood, I studied the dope dealers. I admired how they walked, talked,

dressed, and handled situations.
Being a dope boy was my calling
or being something else is my
calling?

INTERIOR CLASSROOM - DAY

DR. GALE WOOLLEY - Welcome to the
field of nursing. The most
confusing field in healthcare.
Why is nursing confusing? Because
we have so many nursing roles. We
have nursing assistants, licensed
practical nurses, registered
nurses, diploma nurses, associate
nurses, baccalaureate nurses,
nurse practitioners, soon to be
doctorates of nurses. Have you
ever been to a doctor's office
and the person who takes your
blood pressure at the doctor's
office tells you that they will
be your nurse but, on the badge,
you see medical assistant? What
is the role of the nurse? What
does a nurse do? Are you becoming
a nurse for the money? Do you
like working long hours? Are
nurses smarter than doctors?

The woman continues to talk. ANTHONY
sits in class. HE is dressed in a

button up shirt with a tie and little
GIT has on glasses to fit the part. A
long way from the juvenile
correctional facility.

          NARRATOR - I got introduced to
          nursing from MORAN and LENNY, an
          EMT and a paramedic from the
          ambulance job. DR.

          DR. GALE WOOLLEY - I would like
          to share something with you all
          that I learned many years ago.
          Yes, I am old.

The class laughs.

          DR. GALE WOOLLEY - Nursing school
          teaches you the skills and
          knowledge needed to become a
          nurse, but we cannot teach you
          how to care. We can provide you
          with the definition of empathy,
          but we cannot teach you how to
          care. In nursing, you will learn
          that nurses are born and not
          made.

The class is silent.

          DR. GALE WOOLLEY - I can teach
          you how to become a nurse, but I
          cannot teach you how to care. I

want you all to close your eyes
and think of a time that you
helped someone who was in need. I
know a lot of you have past
medical experiences. Do not
reflect on those experiences.
Just think of a time that you
helped someone who was really in
need, and you helped them because
it was the right thing to do, and
you cared about their well-being.

The class follows directions.

DR. GALE WOOLLEY - That is
nursing. Caring for a human
being.

ANTHONY thinks about THE MAN that was
dressed in a hospital gown in Overtown
with the IV pole.

Dr. GALE WOOLLEY leaves the room as
the class were thinking.

INTERIOR GRANNY'S HOUSE - DAY

ANTHONY is sitting talking with
GRANNY.

GRANNY - What?

ANTHONY - Yeah, he played.

GRANNY shakes her head no.

NARRATOR - At the ambulance
station, a paramedic named
ALPIZAR used a picture of a white
woman standing in a village in
Africa with four little black
boys. He wrote Isa the owner of
the company on the white woman
and for each little boy he wrote
the crew names FORBES
(Paramedic), JEAN (Paramedic),
MITCHELL (EMT), and GRAY(EMT) to
indicate that this woman is our
savior rescuing us from poverty
or how we took it she is our
slave master.

GRANNY - I hope that you did not
respond. Because the minute you
do, they will fire your ass.

ANTHONY - I was calm, and I
pretended to laugh it off. It is
messed up that we cannot respond
to their bs without getting into
trouble.

GRANNY - Did they fire him?

ANTHONY - No.

> GRANNY - Then you know where the company stand. Look, baby the more educated you become you will find that it is some ignorant mother fuckers that are in position. I mean some ignorant mother fuckers, but they are in position.

ANTHONY has an expression of anger on his face.

> GRANNY - You must learn to play for position and to box out all the bullshit.

> ANTHONY - I mean GRANNY, we do everything the right way at the job. Why do we have to be subjective to ignorance all the time? I bet if I shoot his ass then they will know where I stand.

GRANNY has tears in her eyes as she cannot respond to ANTHONY.

EXTERIOR AMBULANCE BAY - NIGHT

ANTHONY is finishing up the end of shift. HE submitted the report sheets to the SHIFT COMMANDER (MR. JEAN). HE cleans up the truck and gets in HIS car to go home.

> NARRATOR - I have been in nursing school for over a year now. I was going to school full time and working on the ambulance 36 hours per week. Being busy did not bother me at all. Having a structured life kept me focused and away from the street life.

INTERIOR CAR - NIGHT

ANTHONY receives a call from HIS cousin, MON.

> ANTHONY - YO

> MON - I need you GIT, ASAP fool.

> ANTHONY - Yeah!

> MON - Yeah! They played.

> ANTHONY - Say less.

ANTHONY hangs up the phone. ANTHONY drives to a corner store and buys a black tee shirt and a black skully hat.

> NARRATOR - An ASAP call.

ANTHONY pulls up to his AUNTIE DEAN'S
house. A place where HE once lived.
MON is sitting on the porch waiting on
ANTHONY.

EXTERIOR FRONT PORCH - NIGHT

ANTHONY approaches MON.

ANTHONY - What they do?

MON gives ANTHONY a chopper (AK-47).

MON - Man, GIT these fuck niggaz
played on some hoe shit. I need
you fool.

ANTHONY puts on the black tee shirt
and the skully hat.

ANTHONY - You need me to hit up a
crib fool.

MON - Nah, I upped (pulled the
gun out) on their fuck ass and
they got missing quick. So, I am
waiting on them to slide back
thru.

GIT sits on the porch with the chopper
on his lap. HE thinks about being on
this porch reading bible verses with
JACOB and SETH.

NARRATOR - Jailhouse thinking is
not the same as freedom actions.

A few hours go by. GIT has been on the
porch with MON for about 4 to 5 hours.
The two men are silent as they prepare
to put in work.

NARRATOR - Shootings in the
ghetto have become part of the
culture. It's a part of the G
code that we are born into. You
see the G code is a thing that we
live by and die by. MON is my
blood. How the fuck am I going to
turn my back on a nigga that
provided me with food, clothing,
and shelter when my MAMA left me
when I was fifteen years old. A
nigga that looked out for me when
I ain't had nothing.

MON is smoking on a joint. ANTHONY is
starring at him.

NARRATOR - I do not even know
what this incident is about.

The morning rises and MON releases GIT
from his duties.

MON - Bet that up GIT. Them hoe
ass niggaz don't want shit.

The two men says their goodbyes with a five-handshake hug.

ANTHONY drives to the beach. HE is staring at the ocean while collecting HIS thoughts.

EXTERIOR BEACH - MORNING

ANTHONY is sitting on the hood of HIS car staring at the ocean.

> NARRATOR - Nothing happened. But something did happen to me that night. I put my future at risk. I thought that I had changed. I didn't have the same feeling of holding onto a chopper that I once had a few years ago. I had become someone in life and holding onto that chopper made me realize that I am destine for failure. All the progress that I have made over the past few years could have been washed away in just one night. I would have let GRANNY, my MAMA, TOYA, AALIYAH, my DAD, and the whole hood down. DAMN! Why do I put myself in these fucked up situations?

ANTHONY stares up at the sky. HE makes a promise to himself that HE will be a

voice of change to a population that
accepts prison and death as
normalities.

>NARRATOR - Gun violence is
>standard patterns in the ghetto
>but earning a degree and staying
>positive are not.

A few months go by, and ANTHONY
continues to work on the ambulance and
attend nursing school.

INTERIOR FUNERAL HOME - NIGHT

ANTHONY is side by side with MON at a
wake for BL. Mourning the death of
their friend who was shot and killed.

>NARRATOR - JAMAL GAINER also
>known as BLACK best known as BL,
>my big homie. I had a lot of
>respect for BL. He saved my life
>a few years ago.

ANTHONY reminisces on the night that
HE was on the other end of them
choppers.

EXTERIOR TRAP HOUSE - NIGHT

"Few Years Ago,"

NARRATOR - I was selling dope as a young GIT with BIG JUNE and MIKE in Bunche Park. MIKE got into it with a legend from the Triangle on Ali Baba Avenue in Opa-Locka. Anybody knows about the Bab; knows them niggas don't play. I remember hustling on the side of the house and BIG JUNE came and grabbed the gun from me and told me that he got to watch MIKE'S back. A few minutes past by and I came around to the front of the house, and I saw about five niggas with choppers in their hands, and one of the men was BLACK. BLACK told me to get from around there. One of the men tried to stop me from leaving, but BLACK made sure that I got from around there.

INTERIOR FUNERAL HOME - NIGHT

ANTHONY and MON are looking at BL'S body in the casket.

NARRATOR - Sometime after the incident at the trap, BLACK told me that the only reason that they did not come out of the van

shooting was that MON told them
that I was over there hustling.

ANTHONY looks at MON with a look of
gratitude in HIS eyes.

ANTHONY leaves BL's wake, and heads to
meet up with a few of HIS comrades out
of the Leaf.

EXTERIOR KILLA'S CRIB — NIGHT

ANTHONY is in a room with a few
outlaws including ZAY TWO.

ANTHONY only went to the house because
DAT BOY called HIM crying begging to
stop the beef.

> ZAY TWO - HOUND what are you over
> here for? This ain't no college
> shit nigga.

> ANTHONY - Tighten up fool. I'm
> over here because the nigga
> called me.

> ZAY TWO - What you talking to
> that nigga? That's your homeboy?

> ANTHONY - I don't even know how
> the mark got my number.

ZAY TWO has that look in his eyes.

ANTHONY - DAT BOY said he shot at
the ground he wasn't trying to
hit anybody.

KILLA - But the nigga shot tho.

ANTHONY - Man, he told me that LO
was threatening him, his kids and
shit. He was trying to leave but
niggas came at him, and he shot
at the ground just to get up out
of there.

ZAY TWO - We were on them pills
and shit. Just fucking with him.
He could of took the beaten.

The outlaws laugh. ANTHONY laughs. A
few words exchanged between ANTHONY
and his comrades. ANTHONY decides to
take this opportunity to speak on what
HE learned in nursing school about
prescription drug use.

ANTHONY - Damn dog. Niggas
getting on pills and shit. Y'all
ever heard of the first pass
effect.

KILLA starts to laugh.

KILLA - My nigga GIT HOUND about
to teach and shit. Laughs.

ANTHONY - G shit! The
concentration in the pills y'all
popping can damage the liver
overtime. Plus, the increase in
alcohol consumption can be even
more damaging to the liver. Man,
we are young fool and niggaz
drinking hard liquor daily.

ZAY TWO - It's numb the pain.

ANTHONY is familiar with the
psychological scars that the game of
the street life leaves on its players.

ANTHONY - More pain will exist
when you start to have
withdrawals, seizures and your
liver is damaged. If your liver
gets fucked up, your urine turns
to tea, shit turns to clay, belly
gets big, and a nigga will have
yellow eyeballs.

The outlaws' eyes are on ANTHONY.

ANTHONY - Leave the game and life
can numb the pain.

ANTHONY realizes that the men respect
HIM because HE comes from their
culture and that HE is also in

college, so they take heed to HIS
words.

> ANTHONY - True shit. I'm asking
> on the strength of me that y'all
> spare DAT BOY. I'll let LO know
> that we spared the mark.

> ZAY TWO - How we gonna look if a
> nigga shoots at us, and we ain't
> get back.

ANTHONY remembers the favor that BL
did for HIM and HIS mission to model a
practice on reducing gun violence to
the people that are around HIM that HE
uses this opportunity to speak to room
full of gangsters on encouraging them
to put their guns down.

> ANTHONY - You know you ain't no
> sucker if you busted that bitch
> (gun) before. Why the fuck we
> keep killing one another over
> nothing? Y'all was fucked up
> (drug/alcohol intoxicated) that
> y'all decided to punish a nigga
> that didn't deserve it. DAT BOY
> was scared as fuck that's why the
> mark shot at the ground and ran.

The men laugh.

> ANTHONY - I'm asking on the
> strength of me that we let this
> one slide.

They agreed and ANTHONY made
ratification towards trying to change
the people around HIM.

EXTERIOR MLK METRORAIL STATION -
EVENING

ANTHONY is at the MLK metro rail
station looking at the quotes for
inspiration. HE is approached by UNCLE
JIMMY.

> UNCLE JIMMY - ANT! What's up man?

UNCLE JIMMY has a big smile on his
face. He hugs ANTHONY and the two men
sit down to talk.

> NARRATOR - JIMMY is my DAD'S
> brother. JIMMY is a real smart
> dude, but he felt victim to that
> pipe. His only problem in life
> was that he got hooked on crack.
> That crack ruined his life. He's
> been in and out of prison for
> drug related charges, burglaries,
> and other things. All related to
> his drug use.

ANTHONY - I'm just over here chilling. Gathering my thoughts. Trying to figure shit out.

UNCLE JIMMY - What's happening?

ANTHONY - A lot of bullshit.

UNCLE JIMMY - Drop it on me young blood.

ANTHONY - It's like I'm trying to be three different people.

UNCLE JIMMY nods his head yes.

ANTHONY - I put the glasses on at the schoolhouse on that Urkel vibe. Being sociable and trying to fit in.

UNCLE JIMMY - Entertaining folks.

ANTHONY - Yeah! At the workhouse, I try to be less intimidating. Pick up any call. Volunteer to stay late and to pick up extra shifts. But they love to make black jokes and shit. Make fun of a nigga for doing the right thing. It's like I can't get a break Unc. At the schoolhouse, one of them girls accused me of stealing her tires off her car.

UNCLE JIMMY - Did you take them?

ANTHONY - Hell nah.

UNCLE JIMMY - Laughs. I know you didn't take them. I'm just fucking with you.

ANTHONY - Serious Unc.

UNCLE JIMMY - Welcome to life ANT. You ain't safe no matter where you are at. If you keep striving to better yourself, you have got to learn that life will test you in   every way possible. You are going to have to learn that you must adapt to situations as they come in life.

ANTHONY - I do.

UNCLE JIMMY - I know you are doing it, but the bullshit comes along with life.

ANTHONY - Like in the streets. I thought I was done with the bullshit out there. Then I found myself back with a gun in my hand or around some niggas with some guns.

            UNCLE JIMMY - That's the third
            person.

ANTHONY nods his head yes.

            UNCLE JIMMY - ANTHONY, you made
            it pass that gangster bullshit
            out here. Young blood, you work
            on the ambulance, and you are a
            college student. Where I just
            came from, young niggas are doing
            twenty or better in the joint and
            they'll kill to have a second
            chance at life.

ANTHONY knows that HE has accomplished
so much to let it go down the drain.

            UNCLE JIMMY - You be their second
            chance. Move like you are in the
            joint. Structured your time
            wisely, stay away from the
            bullshit, and when trouble comes
            you strategically handled it.

UNCLE JIMMY pauses.

            UNCLE JIMMY - It's okay to be
            different people in different
            settings. You can't be that Urkel
            mother fucker out here on the
            set. You can't be that street
            nigga on the ambulance truck.

Those three different people make
you ANTHONY. Shit, life dealt you
a hand and you playing your hand
for survival. Whether it's a book
in your hand to study, some
medicine in your hand to save
someone's life, or whether it's a
gun in your hand to show a nigga
you ain't playing. That's your
hand. Accept it as your strength
to survive and strive to be a
better ANTHONY. Obstacles are
going to come at you all the
time. Stick your chest out and
handle it.

UNCLE JIMMY gives ANTHONY dap.

UNCLE JIMMY - The G code.

INTERIOR AUDITORIUM - DAY

Soulful gospel plays.

It is graduation day. The once
GANGSTER IN TRAINING earned his
Bachelor of Science Degree in Nursing
(BSN) from Nova Southeastern
University at the age of twenty-four
years old. Seven years post HIS
incarceration.

DR. WOOLLEY calls the name of ANTHONY
GRAY. ANTHONY is walking across the
stage. HE stops in the middle of the
stage and put up four fingers up.

In the audience:

☐ GRANNY has tears in her eyes as
she remembers the once doubtful
boy who felt that HE was not
college material and now he has
earned a bachelor's degree in
nursing.

☐ SANDY is clapping with a big
smile on her face as she
remembers the many nights of
going to get HIM from the
juvenile detention center.

☐ BOBBY has his four fingers in
the air too as he remembers the
night of the robbery with DAVE.

☐ BIG HOMIE DRE DAWG has his four
fingers in the air as well as he
remembers GIT has a young drug-
dealer listening to Pac in the
trap,

☐ and DAVID is free after serving
seventeen years in prison, and he

comes home to see his lil man earning a bachelor's degree.

NARRATOR – My classmates and people on the stage did not know why I had four fingers, but I'm from Overtown, and I am a Towner 4 Life.

The music stops.

PERFORMANCE

The caring process for ANTHONY GRAY continues with the implementation of HIS performance in becoming a Registered Nurse and a blessing that came from trouble to those around HIM. ANTHONY identifies that HE represents a culture that accepts prison and death as normality for the young in the forms of drug-dealing, substance use and gun violence. As HE learned the different roles of being a Registered Nurse, HE also, performs the role reversals of being a thug and a nerd to maintain HIS survival within HIS culture and the culture of HIS professional environment. ANTHONY utilizes HIS courage to perform a caring act on murder prevention. ANTHONY actions attained the concept that nurses are born and not made as HE creates change within HIS environment by mentoring young teenagers in the street life on the benefits that education has over the drug game.

WHO IS MR. GRAY?

" Every great dream begins with a dreamer. Always remember, you have within you the strength, the patience, and the passion to reach for the stars to change the world. "

- Harriet Tubman

INTERIOR CHURCH — DAY

GRANNY'S funeral.

PASTOR — LILLIAN NEWBOLD THURSTON was born on March 8, 1926. She attained her general education in the segregated Dade County Public Schools. LILLIAN graduated with honors from Booker T. Washington Jr. Senior High School in the class of 1945. She received her teaching education at Kentucky State College and obtained her nursing education as a licensed practical nurse at Hunter College on Park Avenue in New York City. Lillian, in her no-nonsense style, stressed the importance of education to anyone who would listen. As a demonstration of her personal commitment and the desire to update her education for the 21st century, Lillian decided to go back to school after retirement. At the age of 71 years old she enrolled in a bachelor's program at Florida International University where she earned a degree in English; graduating at the age of 73 years old, she was the oldest and proudest member of her graduating class.

The church choir is singing.

As they put GRANNY'S casket in the ground, ANTHONY breaks down crying. HIS AUNTIE BETTY consoles HIM for a while.

> NARRATOR - The last time that I cried was at the age of twelve after my first arrest for throwing a deadly missile (rocks)

at a moving vehicle (a school
bus).

INTERIOR HOSPITAL - DAY

A baby is being born. As the baby
cries, ANTHONY has a joyful look in
his eyes as HE welcomes HIS new baby
boy.

"A year later"

BOSTON, MASSACHUSETTS

EXTERIOR STREET - DAY

Slow music plays.

A snowy cold morning. The snow falls
from the sky. People are shoveling
snow from the cars to the street. Cars
are driving. People are standing at
the bus stop.

INTERIOR PRISON - DAY

ANTHONY is walking into a prison. HE
has flashbacks of the slamming of the
large doors. HE enters the prison's
dorm not as an inmate but as a
Registered Nurse. The inmates look at
the new nurse.

> BOSTON INMATE - This nigga got on
> Js.

The men look at ANTHONY as HE mirrors them as a black male with tattoos.

The music stops.

INTERIOR APARTMENT —AFTERNOON

ANTHONY is playing with JUNIOR, his one-year-old son.

> NARRATOR - After my son was born, his mother and I relationship had faded away. She left Miami and moved back to Boston, and I followed to be closer to my son.

INTERIOR MALL - DAY

ANTHONY is shopping with JUNIOR. HE sits on a bench in the mall with JUNIOR to enjoy a snack. HE noticed the conversation of three BOSTON WHITE MEN.

> BOSTON WHITE MAN #1 - Yeah, niggas be tripping.

> BOSTON WHITE MAN #2 - If a nigga stepped to me at the club, I'll fuck his ass up.

BOSTON WHITE MAN #2 gives WHITE MAN #1 a five handshake.

BOSTON WHITE MAN #3 - Real nigga
shit.

The men continue with their
conversation. ANTHONY has an
aggressive look on HIS face but then
becomes confused because they were
calling themselves real niggas.

BOSTON WHITE MAN #3 - I am a type
of nigga that ain't looking for
it, but if drama comes, I'll
handle it.

BOSTON WHITE MAN #1 - Real nigga
shit.

ANTHONY has a look of confusion. HE
didn't know how to respond with anger
or with laughter.

ANTHONY continues to eat HIS snack
with HIS son.

NARRATOR - What the fuck? They
are calling themselves real
niggas. Laughing. I wish GRANNY
was here to hear this confusion.
Laughing.

"Six years later"

ANTHONY continues to live in Boston
co-parenting with JUNIOR'S mother

while working two to three nursing
jobs at a time, being in JUNIOR'S
life, and ANTHONY has decided to go
back to school to work towards a
master's degree.

INTERIOR APARTMENT - MORNING

ANTHONY is sitting at the computer
desk in the living room studying.
JUNIOR is getting ready for school in
HIS bedroom. JUNIOR is struggling to
put his tie on. HE approaches ANTHONY.

>JUNIOR - DAD (yells).

>ANTHONY - Yea, champ?

>JUNIOR - May you help me with my
>tie please.

ANTHONY has a look of joy on HIS face
when JUNIOR enters the room.

>NARRATOR - When I left Miami, I
>was uncertain of our future. I
>never lived anywhere outside of
>Miami, and everything that I
>knew, and loved were in Miami
>except my lil man. It was the
>best decision that I ever made.
>I've been through too much in
>life to be afraid of life because

I got homeboys doing life. Ya
dig.

ANTHONY is helping JUNIOR with his
tie.

ANTHONY - How many chambers do
the heart have?

JUNIOR - 4.

ANTHONY - Name them.

JUNIOR - Right atrium, right
vent-t

JUNIOR has a puzzled look on his face.

ANTHONY - Ventricle. Good job
champ. Keep going.

JUNIOR - Right ventricle, left
atrium and left ventricle.

ANTHONY - Which side does the
blood enter the heart?

JUNIOR - Right side.

ANTHONY continues to quiz HIS son and
gets him ready for school and drops
him off.

NARRATOR - By the time I was my
son's age, I witnessed a murder,
drug transactions, my DAD was in

prison, and I became a GIT. Now, my son is in private school, he lives in a neighborhood with no gunshots, and his dad is a registered nurse working towards a master's degree.

INTERIOR APARTMENT - NIGHT

ANTHONY is on the phone with his friend, JONIDA.

> JONIDA - I was watching a movie about a guy who sold drugs and now he is a rapper. You should write a book about your life based on the things you told me.

> ANTHONY - Laughs. JONIDA anything that's black your white ass relates to me. Laughing.

> JONIDA - Screw you. Laughing. For real ANTHONY. Your book will be very interesting. Especially, about the bipolar or tripolar personalities you have.

Laughing.

> ANTHONY - Laughing. You know I like to be inconspicuous.

> JONIDA - Laughing. You are very
> hard to read, but I am sure your
> story needs to be heard. You are
> a great nurse, and you have the
> ability to relate to people from
> all walks of life.

ANTHONY never really thought about
sharing HIS story.

ANTHONY thinks about the people in HIS
life and their consequences. HIS
cousin, MON who went to federal prison
on gun charges, BOBBY and DAVE who are
at the same prison together serving
time. ZAY TWO who did a couple of
prison bids. ROC who survived 13
gunshot wounds and now is in federal
custody serving a 30-year sentence on
drug conspiracy charges. BIG HOMIE DRE
DAWG who is serving time in the feds
on drug-related charges, and HIS
father, DAVID who got a second chance
at life and now is working for the
waste management company in Miami.

> NARRATOR - I still to this day
> think about THE MAN that came to
> the trap with the IV pole. He
> told me that I was meant to be
> something better in life. Maybe
> my story will inspire other

youths from the ghettos to be
more than trap stars.

"2020 GLOBAL PANDEMIC"

As the world faces the challenges of
the coronavirus, the once trouble
teenager, Little GIT is now ANTHONY
the nurse, and HE is on the front
lines of the fight helping save lives
in the pandemic.

INTERIOR HOSPITAL — NIGHT

ANTHONY has three jobs as a nurse
during the pandemic. HE works as an
emergency nurse, IV home infusion
nurse, and a medical/surgical nurse.
HE is working an average of 60-72
hours per week between the three jobs.
HIS son is on quarantine with his
mother, and ANTHONY communicates with
him through face time and outside his
bedroom window.

ANTHONY is participating in many
intubated procedures in the emergency
room, HE is at the bedside taking care
of COVID patients on the
medical/surgical unit, and HE is in
the patient's home providing
intravenous infusions. During the
pandemic, the once troubled youth, GIT

HOUND, was also a graduate student, and by GOD'S grace HE has graduated.

INTERIOR ANTHONY'S HOME - EVENING

ANTHONY is giving a speech at a virtual town hall meeting.

> My name is Anthony A. Gray, and I am a graduate student at Southern New Hampshire University (SNHU) in the Master of Science in Nursing (MSN) Program on the Clinical Nurse Leader (CNL) track, and I am proud to say that I am at the end of my journey in the program after three years of studying. I have been a licensed Registered Nurse (RN) for twelve years, and I have worked in a variety of healthcare settings in nursing, including skilled nursing care, sub- acute rehab, correctional nursing, medical-surgical nursing, ambulatory care, detox nursing, mental health nursing, emergency medicine, home care management, home infusion nursing care, and as a clinical instructor.

My future in nursing is to be working in a role as a member of an interdisciplinary team in healthcare aimed at designing and implementing working projects that are geared towards improving healthcare quality and effective decision making for healthcare professionals. As a graduate student, I challenged myself in observing healthcare quality and decision making at different healthcare institutions by being employed as a per-diem clinical nurse at different facilities during the same duration of time period. For instance, in a six-month period on different days out of the week I rotated in different nursing roles as an orthopedic medical surgical nurse at an acute hospital, patient-centered managed home nurse at an ambulatory care clinic, and as a nurse at a detox facility. I was able to observe the benefits and risks in healthcare quality with pain management.

This challenge allowed me to gain experiences and in engage in

projects during the graduate
program on understanding of the
program outcomes by SNHU in
creating client-centered,
culturally appropriate health
prevention and promotional
initiatives that improve the
health, safety, and quality of
life for people and their
communities. The challenge of
being a per-diem nurse allowed me
to compare healthcare quality in
adult wellness at homecare
settings in patient-family
centered care, a magnet hospital
versus a non-magnet hospital, and
intravenous infusions.

As a graduate student, I was
doing very well in the course
grades, and I was able to support
my son with multiple per diem
jobs. Then, the global pandemic
of the coronavirus occurred, and
I was faced with another
challenge of being a graduate
student and a much-needed nurse.
When the global pandemic
happened, I was working as a
clinical staff nurse at an
emergency department (ED), and

the need for my presence increased. I was working an average of sixty to seventy-two hours per week as a per-diem nurse, and my academic focus had declined. I had to become isolated from my son at the beginning stages of the pandemic and found myself unsure if I would ever finish school, or will I catch the deadly virus.

After a month of being unfocused and unsure of the future, I developed new challenges in prioritizing my life. I put my family obligations first, work second, and school third. At this period, I was working on my capstone proposal, obtaining a practice site approval, and meeting the requirements of the Institutional Review Board (IRB) at SNHU for the final course. This period was frustrating, and it took several months to obtain. During this time, I was continuing to work on new personal career challenges in observing healthcare quality in a global pandemic and effective/ineffective decision-making by leadership. During a six-month period, I was working as a per-diem clinical nurse at two different emergency departments, and as a staff nurse on a medical-surgical telemetry unit.

This six-month challenge allowed me to gain the experience in distinguishing the difference between working at a magnet hospital versus a non-magnet hospital, and the role of leadership has in decision-making on patient care. I also was able to understand the importance of the program outcomes by SNHU in model leadership and professional practices in healthcare by building effective working relationships and facilitating ethical and strategic decision making across organizations.

Finally, after months of eight revisions on my capstone proposal, I was approved, and I met all the requirements at SNHU to enter the final course of the graduate program. The course was set to start in three months, and I had three months to enter a new challenge of being a clinical instructor as an adjunct faculty member at a local university. This challenge was amazing, and I am very appreciative of this challenge. The four nursing students that I had the privilege of sharing my nursing insights with provided me with a warm spirit of being a registered nurse, the value of nursing practice, and the importance of using teamwork in the nursing profession.

I am at the end of my journey as a graduate student in a global pandemic, and I would like to give thanks to the faculty at SNHU for guiding me through the MSN program. I am very grateful.

The End.

"A SOUL TO CARE IS TO HAVE THE
COMPASSION AND EMPATHY TO CARE FOR
ANOTHER PERSON'S WELLBEING TO THEIR
BEST INTEREST."

– ANTHONY A. GRAY, MSN RN

GIT HOUND, AGE 38

RIP

Carlos "LOS" Sanchez

Darlene Brown

Dean "BOSS" Green

Eddie Brown Sr.

Frantz "ZAY THREE" Eugene

Jamal "BL" Gainer

James "BIG JUNE" Cook

Lillian "GRANNY" Thurston

Margaret "MS. MARGY" Thomas

Rose "MS. ROSE" Taldon

Special Thanks:

Aaliyah S. Matthews

Albert "BERT" Forbes

Andrew "ANDY" McLellan

Anthony A. Gray, Jr.

Anthony "BIG ANT" Jones

Antonio A. Gray

Barbara Brown

Betty Cook

BLIND

Bobby "OG" Smith

Bridgett "MS. B" Taylor

Brigham and Women's Faulkner Hospital

Carole Ashe

Cassandra "MAMA" Oneil

Chris Mitchell

CLB

Daniel Crowley

David "DAD" Gray

Demond Brown

Dorian L. Bennett

DOUBLE J

Edwin Barbosa

Haley Olsen-Mason

Henry Moran

Fly Supply Clothing

Frank Rodriguez

Dr. Gale Woolley

Geraldine Brown

Gregory "DRE DAWG" Spencer

Jean Wilson

Jimmy Thurston

Jonida Taraj

Joyce Augustine

Lauren Hughes

Latoya D. Gray

Lenny Mora

Lita Thompson

Lynn Reid

Maida Sanders

Mary Beth Hamilton

Marie Fleury

Roger Forbes

Romanila Oliver

Ronald "WOOD" Brunson

Rose "MS. ROSE" Teldon

Tavaris Stinson

Tyriq "RIQ HAVOC" Ramsey

Willie Williams

ZAY TWO

www.ingramcontent.com/pod-product-compliance
Lightning Source LLC
Chambersburg PA
CBHW060615290326
41930CB00051B/2393